DOG
TRAINING
A LIFELONG GUIDE

Top Trainers
Share Their Secrets

by Arden Moore

BOWTIE™
P R E S S

A DIVISION OF FANCY PUBLICATIONS
Irvine, California

Ruth Strother, project manager
Nick Clemente, special consultant
Karla Austin, editor
Michelle Martinez, editorial assistant
Suzanne Gehrls, production manager
Cover design by Michele Lanci-Altomare
Book design by Bocu & Bocu
Illustrations by Kimball Graphics on pages 25, 26, 28, 30, 41,
49, 50, 59, 69, 70, 71, 72, 73, 75, 76, 82, 83, 123, 129, and 130

The dogs in this book are referred to as *he* and *she* in alternating chapters.

Library of Congress Cataloging-in-Publication Data
Moore, Arden.
  Dog training, a lifelong guide : top trainers share their secrets / by
Arden Moore.
      p. cm.
Includes bibliographical references (p.).
  ISBN 1-889540-90-0 (pbk. : alk. paper)
  1. Dogs--Training. I. Title.
  SF431 .M82 2002
  636.7'0887--dc21
                                              2002005337

BowTie™ Press
A DIVISION OF FANCY PUBLICATIONS
3 Burroughs
Irvine, California 92618

Printed and Bound in Singapore
10 9 8 7 6 5 4 3 2 1

✦ ✦ ✦ ✦ ✦ ✦ ✦ ✦ ✦

To all the delightful dogs that remind us to laugh, play, and take an occasional well-deserved afternoon nap. Special mention goes to Crackers, my childhood family dog, and Jazz, my Corgi chum.

CONTENTS

INTRODUCTION

Dear Dog Lover:

Dogs aren't equipped with built-in foolproof training manuals. In fact, it may be easier to wire your new stereo system than fine-tune your dog. Fortunately, you are in luck. In *Dog Training, a Lifelong Guide*, you receive a unique opportunity to learn gentle no-punish training methods from five of the world's top dog trainers. I am proud to showcase the positive training methods of Debi Davis, Donna Duford, Susan Garrett, Terry Ryan, and Sue Sternberg. After careful research, I selected them because each proves day after day that you can teach dogs in fun, positive ways without physical force.

This book is divided into five chapters. Each chapter covers positive reinforcement training methods and profiles a world-renowned trainer. Each trainer's profile is located at the beginning of her respective chapter, allowing you to peek into her life by reading about her journey into the dog training profession and how she honed her special training techniques.

The true beauty of this book is that many of these training tips and insights are relevant to all dogs. For example, even though you may not require a service dog, the service dogs chapter offers terrific clicker training tips that you can use on your family dog. Not only will you find a lot of training terms within the main text but you can also refer to the book's appendices for a list of defined terms.

As dog lovers, we will always be involved in the different stages of a dog's life, from adopting a new dog to raising a puppy to caring for an older dog. Maybe you want to get involved in a dog sport or want a well-trained dog who can fetch the TV remote or help pull clothes out of the dryer. You will read how even tiny dogs can make giant strides as service dogs. You will discover how to stop your dog from digging in your garden by practicing the art of compromise. You will learn why the circular tail wag is such a key sign to look for when adopting a shelter dog. You will recognize why puppy kindergarten classes are so crucial to the social development of your new tail-wagging pal. And you will gain inside secrets on how to turn your jock dog into a ribbon-winning performance athlete. This is the book you've been looking for—a continual reference for the different stages of your dog's life. It's not intended to be read just cover to cover but, rather, chapter by chapter. You get to pick and choose when and what information is relevant to you.

Face it, we love our dogs—even when they chew up our favorite pair of leather shoes or tip over the kitchen trashcan. But proper doggy etiquette is within your reach. It starts with proper training. Read on and let our talented trainers guide you and your dog to a healthier, happier relationship.

Paws up!

—Arden Moore

SHELTER DOGS: FINDING A PERFECT MATCH FOR YOU

Profiled Trainer: Sue Sternberg

Sue Sternberg was four years old the day her parents returned from the veterinary clinic without Pepita, the family's beloved standard schnauzer. She saw their reddened eyes, heard their sobs, and knew without a word being spoken that Pepita wasn't coming back. "Pepita had an incurable skin problem and had to be euthanized at age two," recalls Sue. "It was the first time that I saw my parents cry."

Dogs were bestowed full-fledged family member status in the Sternberg's New York City household so it didn't take long for the family to adopt a dog like Pepita, this time a black Labrador-mix ("my parents liked the name—it means little pebble in Spanish"), and Minnie, a dachshund. Both dogs lived well into their teens.

Sue's mom, Norma, worked as a leading pediatric oncologist, developing treatment protocols and improving survivor rates among cancer-stricken children. Her father, Stephen, preferred behind-the-scenes research as a top pathologist. Both are retired and maintain close contact with Sue and her sister,

PHOTO BY JEAN M. FOGLE

Alessandra, a clinical psychologist. "My parents are passionate people who are very inspirational to me," says Sue. "Everyone else in my family has multiple college degrees but me. My mother encouraged me to do what I wanted and never to do it on a small scale. My parents have never said that they were disappointed that I did not become a doctor."

When it comes to shelter animals, Sue is the modern Doctor Doolittle. She is good at read-

"Our goal is to bring the shelter to the people, instead of waiting until it's too late when people are bringing their animals to the shelter." — SUE STERNBERG

ing a dog's body language (she can tell that a circular tail wag is far friendlier than a high-over-the-back stiff wag), deciphering a dog's temperament, and identifying good matches between adopters and shelter dogs. Arguably, she ranks as the top trainer of shelter dogs in the country. Sue began as a dog control officer, switched to an obedience trainer, and is now a dog behavioral expert, shelter consultant, and kennel operator.

Sue credits the late but great Ramona, a shelter dog she adopted, for guiding her toward her career. Ramona, tells Sue, was part of a litter headed for certain death by a frustrated breeder of Great Danes. It turns out a neighborhood black Labrador retriever mated with the breeder's champion bloodline Great Dane, resulting in a batch of crossbred puppies. But when the litter arrived at a local shelter, a shelter worker took them home to foster. When Sue, who was working as an animal control officer at another

shelter, came to visit, Ramona was the last puppy available for adoption. "The second I saw her, I knew I had to have her. She didn't effusively wag her tail, but there was a chemical connection between us," recalls Sue. "Ramona was my first dog as an adult, a once-in-a-lifetime dog who lived to be thirteen years old."

Ramona paved the way for the six adopted or found-as-strays dogs with people-sounding names who now reside with Sue. She runs down the canine crew:

- **Larry:** "He's a thirteen-year-old French bull-dog from the American Society for the Prevention of Cruelty to Animals (ASPCA) in New York City. He can be intense, a real fireball that gets aroused around most dogs. And, well, he *looks* like a Larry."
- **Vinnie:** "He's an eight-year-old German shepherd my friends found in Queens, running down the street dragging a chain. Vinnie is outgoing with a great temperament, and I

named him after my friend who found him."

- **Carmen:** "She is my soul mate, this five-year-old half Rhodesian Ridgeback, half Doberman pinscher-mix, I guess. I drove her home from a nearby shelter and she sat in the front seat and just stared at me. Within twenty minutes, she put her paw on my shoulder. It's as if she knew she had found heaven."

- **Dorothy:** "We connected the day I saw her at a shelter in Kansas. But I flew back to New York. Two weeks later, she was still at the shelter and four weeks later, after sending for her, she arrived at La Guardia Airport into my open arms. Naturally, with her being from Kansas, I named her after Dorothy in the *Wizard of Oz*."

- **Beatrice:** "She gave me that sweet, soft look when I was conducting a shelter workshop in Ardmore, Oklahoma. I adopted her, but she broke with distemper and almost died. My guess is that she is half cattle dog, half Border collie-mix."

- **Hop Sing:** "I'm spending three days vacationing at a ranch in Utah and notice this cattle dog puppy. His owner, a cowboy, said the puppy 'didn't have no instinct' and asked if I

wanted him. So, I vacationed with Hop Sing, took him on hikes, and of course, fell in love. Talk about your souvenirs."

Sue travels coast to coast, working with big shelters, little shelters, public ones, and private ones, introducing ways to help increase their adoption rates. She also lectures to dog trainers and dog lovers at workshops, always in her down-to-earth, startle-you-but-teach-you style.

At a recent American Association of Pet Dog Trainers national conference in San Diego, a wall-to-wall crowd squeezed into one of the larger rooms to hear her speech. She arrived with a grin on her face, donned in a catch-your-eye, red-and-white polka dot dress. The minute she took the microphone, she had her audience mesmerized, amused, and attentive.

Sue willingly takes on more crusades. In a true Charles Kuralt travel-down-the-back roads style, she recently created the Training Wheels Outreach Program in which shelter workers and trainers travel in vans throughout rural communities, meeting dog owners, donating free pet supplies, and offering free training advice. Eventually, she envisions a national on-the-road program that uses neighborly advice to help owners be better guardians to their dogs. "Our goal is to bring the shelter to the people, instead of waiting until it's too late when people are bringing their animals to the shelter," explains Sue. "We want to intervene early enough so that a puppy or adult dog doesn't end up chained outside or relegated to an outdoor pen, and we want to interrupt the cycle of pet overpopulation by spaying females before they become pregnant."

As she talks, she starts to smile as she recognizes that in her own distinct way she, too, is carrying on the Sternberg family tradition. "My parents taught me to think big and change the world for the better," says Sue. "It took me a long time to realize just how I could contribute. We are literally saving lives—and improving the quality of lives with this mobile outreach program."

Introduction

You decide to adopt a dog—not a puppy—from your local animal shelter. As you walk past the cages of barking, prancing, tail-wagging candidates, you realize looks can be deceiving: That cutie may turn into a Cujo when you get home. How can you find a personality-plus pooch who is perfect for you? Look for the circular wag, ignore the dog for two minutes, and test the dog with cat food—these are some of the foolproof personality tests devised by Sternberg. Her mission: Help shelter workers and potential pet adopters recognize the true temperaments of homeless dogs.

Leading veterinarians like Leslie Sinclair,

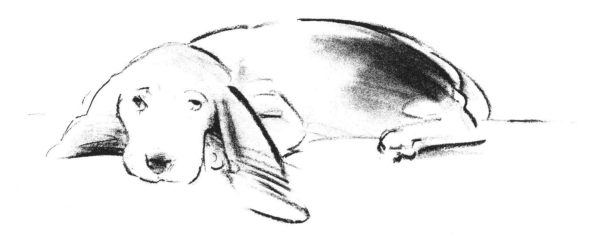

D.V.M., former director of veterinary issues for companion animals for the Humane Society of the United States, now in private practice in Montgomery Village, Maryland, has attended Sternberg's shelter training lectures since 1992. "Sue is one of the best trainers I've seen at correctly observing and interpreting a dog's body posture and facial expressions. She is amazing," says Dr. Sinclair.

By identifying a dog's true intentions from his body and vocal cues, potential dog owners can ensure a perfect—and safe—match, says Sternberg, who also operates Rondout Valley Kennels, a boarding kennel and separate animal shelter in Accord, New York. "Don't kid yourself—some dogs at shelters are downright dangerous," she warns.

In fact, Sternberg says that the ability to know which shelter dogs are wonderful and which ones are problem-filled could easily be the eighth true wonder of the universe. Sternberg often spends full days at shelters, observing the behaviors of the dogs. "I realize that the only time shelter dogs see people is for an excitable activity: cleaning time, feeding time, leash walks, and public viewing," she notes. "The longer a dog stays in a shelter, in general, the more he learns that the presence of people means time for hyperactivity and arousal."

To help avert incompatible unions between

owners and dogs, Sternberg offers a practical, step-by-step guide to adopting a shelter dog. The first step begins with you, the soon-to-be dog owner.

Phase 1: Do a Self-Assessment

Why are you adopting a shelter dog? To save a life? A noble notion but not very practical. "Never go to the shelter with the idea of feeling like a hero by rescuing a dog nobody else wants," says Sternberg. "You'll only set yourself up for problems down the road. Go in with the attitude that you want to select a really great dog. Take your time and be choosy. After all, this is a pet that may be with you for ten, twelve, or more years."

Assess yourself honestly to determine if you are even a candidate to be a dog owner. Answer the following:

- Do you work long hours, come home, and just want to plop in the chair?
- Do you travel a lot for work, spending days, even weeks away from home?
- Do you want a dog for companionship or protection?
- Do you live in an apartment or a house?
- Do you have a fenced-in yard or a nearby park that permits dogs?
- Are you willing to take your dog on daily long walks?
- Will you groom and bath your dog regularly?

- Can you afford a dog, providing him with food, pet supplies, and medical attention?
- Can you accept a dog snoozing on your sofa?
- Will your weekend plans include activities with your dog?

You should want a dog for companionship and not to guard your prized family heirloom vase or expensive stereo system—that's why home alarm systems were invented. Just having a dog in your home will deter most small-time thieves, but a dog's role in the home should be as a member of the household and not solely as a four-legged burglar alarm. Dogs require a lot of time and responsibility so you want to be sure you are up to the task before you adopt.

Now, make a mental picture of your ideal dog based on personality, not looks. After all, a dog's size, age, gender, and physical markings, which are all important, are not as critical as a dog's temperament. Ask yourself:

• Who is your favorite dog in the world and why?

• What is the dog's personality like?

• How old is this dog?

• What does the dog look like?

• What do you envision your dog doing when you arrive home?

Phase 2: Visit a Shelter

A shelter's geographical location can often provide helpful clues in your search for a dog. It would be nice if all shelters conducted detailed temperament evaluations on all dogs prior to placing them in adoption kennels, but that is not reality. Shelters located near, or in, large urban areas tend to house a higher proportion of dogs who are dominant, aroused, and dangerous. In an urban area, it is a good idea to seek out either a shelter that has a behavioral counselor on staff or a shelter that thoroughly evaluates each dog's temperament. Many rural shelters see a higher percentage of social, submissive, and sweet family dogs.

Keep in mind that there are traditional shelters and no-kill shelters. Traditional shelters euthanize behaviorally unadoptable dogs deemed dangerous before they euthanize the more adoptable ones. No-kill shelters often pride themselves on keeping dogs until they can be placed in homes. Unfortunately, dogs who live in shelters for extended periods of time become more withdrawn or aggressive, making them far less adoptable. Look for warning signs that indicate the quality of a dog's life has diminished: dogs who spin, pace, rebound off kennel walls, lick excessively, develop pressure sores or calluses, or cover themselves in their own excrement.

The majority of dogs at shelters are typically six to eighteen months old—better known as the "teenage years." These are dogs who have outgrown their puppy cuteness. Many are surrendered because they jump up on their owner, yank on the leash, escape the yard, and simply test their owner's limits. Fortunately, a growing number of shelters recognize this and are working with adolescent dogs to improve their adoptability by teaching them basic commands, such as *sit*, *come*, *stay*, and *down*. Graduates of these in-house shelter programs have a greater

chance of being adopted because they display their new good manners.

If you have children, leave them at home when you schedule time to make your first shelter visit. You need to make sure a dog passes the temperament test before introducing him to your children. You don't want to let your child's, *Let's get this dog, Daddy*, pleadings influence you emotionally so that you make the wrong selection. Once you've narrowed down your choice to two or three dogs, then bring your children to meet the finalists. As a general rule, do not adopt a dog who is over two years of age if you have a family unless that dog was raised as an indoor pet with children and behaved well around them. Children are the number one group of people bitten by dogs, so your selection is very important. If you are unsure about selecting a dog, consider having a knowledgeable shelter worker, experienced trainer, or animal behaviorist accompany you to the shelter.

Phase 3: Meet the Canine Candidates

Once you arrive at the shelter, go in with a high-standard attitude. Never cut any dog a break, and don't make excuses for undesired—especially aggressive—behaviors. If a dog growls or lunges at you, even once, walk away. Also, rule out any dog who is unable to calm down after the first minute of meeting you. "Some call this approach tough love," says Sternberg. "I call it finding a safe match." Limit your attention to dogs who are six months of age or older. You will be able to gain a better picture of a dog's true temperament once he has completed puppy hood as many fearful behaviors or dominant issues don't surface until a dog is six months or older.

Not every dog comes with a complete history. Unfortunately, many dogs are picked up as strays, their backgrounds remaining mysteries. So, obtain as much factual information from the shelter staff as possible regarding the dog's age, breed or mix, and gender. Ask if the dog has bitten or nipped anyone before. If he has, absolutely do not adopt this dog, stresses Sternberg. If the dog was a family pet, ask the shelter staff why the dog was surrendered. But be careful, often surrender-owner history can be full of euphemisms and actually steer you wrong. So often the dog that is turned in due to "allergies" or because the family is "moving" is actually a dog with an aggression problem, which is why evaluating the dogs temperament is so important.

Evaluating a shelter dog's temperament—or any dog that you plan to adopt—can be tricky and there are no absolute guarantees that a dog will always behave kindly in any situation. Dogs, just like people, can react differently to different stresses. You can, however, improve your odds of making a good selection by using the following sociability test.

TWELVE-STEP SOCIABILITY TEST

1. Walk casually through the entire shelter, taking note not to ignore the dogs in the back of the shelter. Don't be influenced by a dog's size, breed, age, or markings. Only focus on his behavior and personality. Look at every dog, scratching off any dog from your list of possibilities who refuses to approach the front of the cage to greet you, lunges at you, bares his teeth, or won't stop barking and jumping, even to greet you.

2. Approach all dogs who readily come to the front of the cage to greet you. Smile, give a little sweet talk, and extend your hand. The ideal dog will jump up in a friendly manner, trying to sniff or lick your hand. Look for a dog displaying slightly squinty eyes, a full circular wag, or one who places the side of his body against the front of the cage to give you as much of his body to pet as possible. These are all friendly signs.

3. Narrow down your candidates to two or three. Ask the shelter worker if you can interact with each dog—one at a time—in a get-acquainted room, a room that is quiet and free from as many distractions as possible so that you and the dog can focus on getting to know each other.

4. Enter the room first and remain standing. When the dog enters, ignore him for a full two minutes. Within two minutes or less, a truly friendly dog will nudge you or gently paw you to gain your attention. If the dog ignores you, heads for the door, or is so distracted by the indoor environment that he never focuses on you, don't adopt him. There is no such thing as a sweet, *aloof* dog.

5. Next, sit down in a chair and ignore the dog for another two minutes. The best candidates will come right over and try to nuzzle next to you, sit between your legs, rub up against you, or even try to join you in the chair. Rule out any dog who continues to sniff the environment and acts like you don't exist. And disqualify any dog who jumps up on your lap with his paws simply to get a better view of things. This dog is "using" you for his own gain—a better perch.

6. Stand up and without saying a word, slowly stroke the dog from the back of his neck to the base of his tail. Pause and repeat the stroking motions two more times. By pausing in between strokes, you are giving the dog the opportunity to predict what will happen next and the choice to accept or avoid your stroking. An adoptable dog should crave attention, wanting to be touched. He should come closer, perhaps even stand on his tippy toes or turn around to get closer to you. You may notice his ears relax and that he is trying to make soft eye contact with you. Disregard any dog who stiffens his muscles, jerks, stops wagging his tail, or backpedals away from you when being touched.

7. Sit down and call the dog over to you. He should respond immediately. Spend twenty seconds sweet talking, petting, and engaging in affectionate interaction with the dog. An ideal dog will be calmed by your touch and respond with gentle acceptance. Rule out an overly excited or highly anxious dog, a dog displaying dilated pupils, a dog with his tail very high over his back, or any dog trying to mouth your hand. These are signs of dominance aggression or fearfulness.

8. Perform this next step only if you are confident that the dog candidate is calm and not aggressive. Test the dog's level of tolerance by examining his teeth, five times for five seconds apiece. This step is necessary to see how tolerant and easygoing the dog will be when you make him do something that he doesn't necessarily want to do. Do not perform this *next* step until the previous steps have indicated, without hesitation, that the dog has been very

A well-tempered dog will promptly greet you.

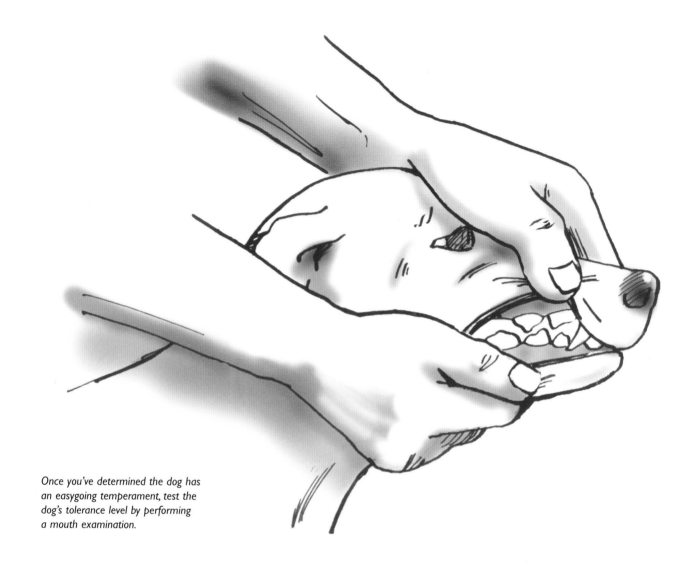

Once you've determined the dog has an easygoing temperament, test the dog's tolerance level by performing a mouth examination.

social and affectionate with you. Place one hand over the top of the dog's muzzle and the other hand under his chin. Part the dog's lips to expose the front and side teeth on one side of his mouth. The dog's mouth should remain closed unless he is heavily panting. Count slowly to five and watch the dog's reaction. Look for a dog that doesn't try to get away from you. The best candidate will try to get even closer or snuggle up against you. Stop the mouth exam if the dog becomes mouthy, growls, snarls, or will simply not tolerate having his teeth examined five times in a row.

9. To test the dog for overly protective feelings about food or toys, have him take a medium to large biscuit out of your hand, following him if he moves to eat it. The best dog will settle at your feet or stay by your side while munching the snack, increasing his tail wagging the closer you get, or drop his toy to say hello if you call him over. The worst candidates are those who growl or stare at you through the corner of their eyes in a defensive posture.

10. Once the dog passes the biscuit test, it's time to further determine the food-guarding potential of the dog. Empty an entire can of cat food on a plate (cat food is full of aroma and definitely a top treat among dogs). While he is eating, walk over, praise him, and watch his body language. If the dog tenses or growls with you nearby, he has flunked. If he eats faster, wags his tail, stops to greet you, or welcomes your stroking, he has high sociability. While he is eating, slowly move your hand toward his bowl, and then, before actually getting

too close, pull back sharply as if scared. Repeat three times. If this elicits any growling, hard staring, or snapping, or if it causes the dog to move to block you from the bowl, he has flunked.

11. Head outside with the dog on a leash. After five minutes of allowing the dog to get used to the area, go to the bathroom, and burn off some energy, you're ready to test his play and prey responses. Take a soft cloth toy or rope toy. Look for a dog who engages in play or is difficult to engage in play but plays lightly and gently. Stop playing and place the toy out of the dog's reach. An adoptable dog should be able to forget about the toy within thirty seconds and be able to reengage in petting and focus on you. Don't choose a dog who growls, plays intensely or furiously, whines, or refuses to share his toy during playtime.

12. Finish the adoption test by interrupting the dog from sniffing about by clapping your hands together to make a loud sound. If the dog is sniffing an object outdoors, sharply clap your hands once from behind the dog, and yell, "Hey!" This step helps you gain a

better understanding as to how responsive this dog will be to your voice. An emotionally sensitive dog will react to your raised voice and sharp sounds by stopping the behavior immediately and turning toward you with ears back and soft, squinty eyes. He also may nudge you, trying to make gentle eye contact or sit tucked in between your legs for acceptance. These dogs are generally easier to live with and train. An aggressive dog may turn around and growl or snap at you. Stay away from adopting a dog who ignores you.

To test a shelter dog's responsiveness outside, sharply clap your hands once from behind him.

Phase 4: Introducing the Shelter Dog to Your Family Dog

If you're looking for a shelter dog to be a playmate for your loyal family dog, an introduction on neutral turf is essential before you sign those adoption papers.

Bring your family dog to the shelter and make the introduction outside in an open area.

Take hold of the leash attached to your dog and have a friend or shelter worker hold the leash of the potential adoptee dog. Initially, keep plenty of space between each dog. Don't walk them directly toward each other. Rather, walk them in parallel paths, slowly merging into a "V" until they are within butt-sniffing range of each other (this is the way dogs intro-

An introduction between a shelter dog and your family dog on neutral turf provides a safe environment.

duce themselves). Keep loose leads as they check each other out, but don't let the leashes tangle. If they behave, bring both dogs indoors, always letting the family dog walk into the room first. This serves as a key signal to the shelter dog that, at least for now, the family dog ranks higher in the pack.

Sit down and quietly watch the two dogs interact. Some dogs bond within seconds, minutes, or hours. Others take weeks, even months. How quick and how strong the friendship bond develops depends on the two dogs. Don't assume or expect love at first sight. Quite often, the best doggy relationships begin with the family dog either growling or snubbing and ignoring the prospective dog. The family dog should not be disciplined, punished, or yelled at for growling at the prospective dog. The best relationships are ones that have a clear distinction in rank hierarchy: A crabby family dog, along with a prospective dog who accepts his lower ranking, can be the best introduction.

Don't be offended if the two dogs get lost in playing together and temporarily forget about you. That's also a good sign. However, be a lit-tle cautious if the shelter dog immediately starts to push, nudge, snarl, or growl in an attempt to get your family dog away from you. This scenario is acceptable only if the family dog asserts himself and the prospective dog acquiesces. Unless, of course, you have a "weenie" dog and are looking to adopt a strong leader-type dog. Otherwise, you're witnessing a duel for the title of dominant dog of the household.

Finally, once you've adopted the new dog and brought him home, give your family dog some slack in his behavior. Don't interfere if the family dog growls, snarls, or even charges (without biting or scratching) the newcomer. The family dog is showing rank and dominance, which is normal and good. Don't yell at or discipline your family dog during this I'm-the-boss display. You'll deliver the wrong message to both dogs. Your family dog may interpret this as you wanting the new dog to rule. The new dog may think you want him to step up his role and exercise more dominance. As a consequence, confusion and aggression may arise between the two dogs, which, without human interference, they often work out fairly well themselves.

WELCOME TO PUPPY PARADISE

Profiled Trainer: Donna Duford

As a five-year-old, Donna Duford couldn't understand why the family dog, a beagle, wasn't allowed inside the house. But the dog's name, Puddles, provided the explanation. "My parents couldn't figure out how to house-train her. She kept peeing in the house, so they built her a wooden doghouse with a tar paper roof for her to live outside," recalls Donna, who grew up on a 15-acre farm in Hooksett, New Hampshire. "I remember how happy Puddles would be to see me when I would visit her. I would take her for walks—or rather, she would walk me—and I remember falling face down in the snow and being dragged a bit but never letting go of her leash."

Donna's parents, Donald and Virginia, now retired, operated the family farm. In addition, her dad operated a construction company while her mom ran a convenience store. "My parents instilled a sense of hard work, personal responsibility, and community responsibility," says Donna. "My dad taught me to get up on

PHOTO BY DANA CREVLING

your feet when you get knocked down in life and how perseverance pays off. My mother taught me about kindness for other people and animals. Our chores had to be done before dinner and the animals on our farm had to be fed first before we ate."

As the second youngest of six kids, Donna's animal-related job was to care for the family's rabbits. "When I was a little girl, my big fantasy was to be the person who could walk into the woods and have all the animals approach me and intrinsically trust with me," she says. She

"Puppies aren't born with perfect manners. They need to be taught appropriate behaviors." — DONNA DUFORD

would stage funerals for dead mice, moles, and any critter she would find, burying them in a little cemetery filled with sweet-smelling lilac bushes. As she grew up, she developed an unspoken rapport with many dogs.

She credits a puppy for fostering and honing her rapport with animals. A strange blend of beagle and sheltie, this twelve-week-old puppy was weaving in and out of traffic in the busy streets of Manchester, New Hampshire. The puppy seemed blissfully happy, not heeding the "Come here!" shouts from her frustrated owner, who tossed his hands in the air and cursed her for not staying by his side. At the time, Donna was working as a dog groomer. Sensing that this was not a good match—for the puppy or the man—she got word to him that she would adopt the puppy if he no longer wanted her. He walked into her shop and told her, "Here, you take her."

Looking back, Donna said, "He didn't understand that the things that were making

him mad are what puppies naturally do: chew, not always come when called, and wander." Suddenly, Donna found herself holding a wiggling puppy with a pluming tail and fuzzy ears. She named her, Maco. Donna quickly learned how to channel Maco's playful puppy spirit into appropriate behavior as the pair found success in training classes—Maco learned it was more fun to be by Donna's side than to run away. Maco lived to be nearly fourteen years old. "Maco got me into dog training and turned out to be a once-in-a-lifetime special soul to me," says Donna.

Today, Donna shares her home in San Francisco, California, with Jett, a nine-year-old Border collie, and Chie, a ten-year-old petit basset griffon vendeen. Jett enjoys honing his herding instincts by corralling Chie in big open spaces while Chie prefers to sniff around hunting for squirrels and rabbits. "The two of them have worked out who controls what in the household, and they love to greet one another

if they have been apart during the day," notes Donna. "I love watching them at mealtimes. If Chie finishes her bowl first, she will try to nudge Jett out to finish his bowl. If there are only vegetables left in his bowl, he permits her, but if it is something more valuable to him like chicken, no way."

Studying and deciphering dog behavior comes naturally for Donna, who has risen from the ranks of part-time dog groomer to an internationally sought-after professional dog trainer, behavioral counselor, and instructor. She served as codirector of the Tufts University School of Veterinary Medicine's exclusive dog training program and taught at the Anglo-American Dog Trainer's and Instructor's Course, in England, before creating the Companion Dog Training Program in 1996. Her lectures at Association of Pet Dog Trainers conferences often result in standing-room-only audiences. She even earned the association's highest rated lecture score in 1998.

"My dad told me that persistency and hard work will pay off and it has for me," she says. Donna, age thirty-eight, looks at her itinerary that will keep her "insanely busy" for the next eighteen months, but she has no regrets. There are dog camps to teach, consultations with dog owners about behavioral problems to perform, and classes on how to perform the right moves in musical canine freestyle to conduct.

"I feel incredibly lucky to be able to earn a living doing something I love," says Donna. "On good days, I get to improve the lives of dogs and people. On great days, I get to save dogs from being euthanized by correcting their behavioral problems so that they can remain in their homes."

Introduction

It's never too early to learn—especially for a puppy. And, learning should always be fun and engaging, says Duford. "Puppies aren't born with perfect manners. They need to be taught appropriate behaviors," says Duford. Her four-prong puppy game plan encompasses educating people, teaching puppies, promoting socialization, and introducing fun tricks. Duford's main message: Have a positive purpose when you play with your puppy, and be her tour guide to your world.

In many ways, puppies are like four-legged computer databanks, lapping up knowledge with each tail-wagging step. The more you arrange for them to experience pleasant and happy circumstances, the more they will develop into contented, well-adjusted adults. By making learning fun and positive, you reduce the likelihood of having to contend with serious behavioral problems when your puppy gets older.

Enroll in Puppy 101

Before you can train a puppy, you need to do a little homework to find out what makes a puppy tick. All puppies follow a pattern of social, physical, and cognitive development during the first twelve to eighteen months of life. Although the timing of these stages varies slightly—depending on factors such as breed and size—they can help identify a puppy's physical and social development.

AGE ZERO TO TWO MONTHS

Physical Growth. For the first two weeks, puppies have only three senses: touch, taste, and smell—they can't see or hear. A puppy sticks close to her mother because her body is still too immature to regulate her own body temperature. By four weeks, baby teeth begin emerging through the gums. At this age, a pup masters the ability to stand, crawl, take a few unsteady steps, and wag her tail.

Social Growth. During the first month, puppies spend 90 percent of their time sleeping. They make a high-pitched sound (ultrasound) their mother can detect but people can't. The only social interaction at this time is with their mother. During the second month, littermates start learning how to play and inhibit their bites.

AGE TWO TO THREE MONTHS

Physical Growth. By eight weeks, most puppies have a full set of baby teeth that enable them to eat regular food. Their motor skills accelerate as they master walking, running, rolling, and playful wrestling. Their neuromuscular system develops by twelve weeks so that puppies have more control of their bladder. This is helpful when people begin to house-train their puppies outside.

Social Growth. The best time to teach doggy etiquette is between the ages of seven and twelve weeks. Everything puppies see, hear, smell, and feel at this age makes lasting impressions and impacts how they behave and react to situations as adults. Expose your puppy to as many positive experiences as possible. Make the trip to the veterinarian pleasant by having the veterinary staff provide treats for your puppy—especially during inoculations—as a positive distraction to receiving an injection. Refrain from subjecting your puppy to any elective surgery that can be painful or traumatic during this time.

Timely Training Tips. Get physical with your puppy—in a good way. Gently and frequently touch her ears, paws, and belly, and examine her mouth. These touches will make trips to the veterinarian's office far less traumatic—for the both of you! Introduce your puppy to different types of slick surfaces such as linoleum or wood floors. Play with her and give her treats. Gauge her reactions. When she appears confident, hoist her up onto a higher surface such as the top of your washing machine, but first place a towel on top of the washer so your puppy will be more comfortable during her first experience of heights. Then if she appears okay, remove the towel so she can get used to a slick, high surface (the slick surface and height resembles a veterinary exam table). Expose your puppy to a lot of different people, different settings (car rides, a friend's home), and different stimuli (vacuum

Place your puppy on a washing machine to simulate a vet's examining table.

cleaner noise, kitchen cooking smells, and friendly older dogs). Enroll your puppy in a kindergarten class that offers socialization in a positive, structured setting. At the same time, teach your puppy these basic behaviors: *sit*, *down*, *come*, and *stay*. (Please see later in this chapter for step-by-step instructions.)

AGE THREE TO SIX MONTHS

Physical Growth. Most small and medium breeds reach 90 percent of their physical stature by six months, but large and giant breeds continue to grow in weight and height. By six months, some puppies can sleep through the night or have the bladder control to go six hours without needing to urinate. Some male puppies have the physical muscle and coordination to be able to lift a leg to urinate. Permanent teeth begin emerging at five months, creating a need to chew to relieve gum discomfort.

Social Growth. Often nicknamed the juvenile stage, puppies during this three-month period are full of energy and excitement—and they are easily distracted. Your puppy is strengthening her friendship bond with you, but at the same time feels more confident to explore her environment on her own. Puppies start to identify where they rank in social settings with other dogs and people. Their play becomes more sophisticated as they practice behaviors they will need as adults. In addition to chasing and wrestling, you may start to see more mounting, pushing, and play growling. Provide a positive play structure and establish yourself clearly as the household leader so that your puppy feels comfortable and secure.

Timely Training Tips. Practice patience and understanding. During this developmental period, your once-responsive puppy may temporarily forget simple learned behaviors, such as *come*, *sit*, or *stay*. Be careful opening doors and maintain control of the leash during walks because some puppies at this age like to get loose and explore, ignoring your calls to come back. Limit training sessions to ten to fifteen minutes because puppies have short attention spans and get bored easily. Making the sessions fun encourages them to learn. Always reward appropriate behavior with praise and food treats. During this juvenile age, teach your dog impulse control by introducing the cues *leave it* and *sit*. (Please see later in this chapter for step-by-step instructions.)

Practice having your puppy *sit* and *stay*, waiting for you to tell her it's okay to approach the food bowl to help her realize that you are in charge of the food dispensing. This helps establish you as household leader.

AGE SIX TO NINE MONTHS

Physical Growth. Most puppies during this age enter a second intensive chewing phase. They also continue to grow in height, and their sexual organs are fully developed so that they can mate.

Social Growth. During this adolescence age, puberty and sexual maturity begin. Females usually experience their first estrus (heat cycle) unless spayed, and males develop the sexual hormone testosterone in sufficient

enough levels to mate. An intact male (a male that has not been neutered) may scent mark by urinating in the house or on the trees along your daily walk to alert other dogs of his presence. Some males may engage in rougher play with other male dogs because testosterone tends to make them more aggressive than female dogs.

Timely Training Tips. If you haven't already, have your puppy spayed or neutered. Redirect your puppy's high energy level into interactive, fun learning games and activities. Enroll your puppy in a formal training class to reinforce basic behaviors, and step up your impulse-control exercises. Introduce your puppy to dog parks, beaches, and other canine-friendly places.

AGE NINE TO TWELVE MONTHS

Physical Growth. By their first birthday, most puppies finish their skeletal growth and look like adults in physique. But they are still developing their intelligence and maturity level.

Social Growth. Welcome to the "terrible twos," an apt nickname because many puppies behave like unruly human toddlers. At this age, some puppies may test their limits and even challenge their own abilities. Some may not come immediately when called because they are too distracted playing with other dogs or toys. Some puppies begin barking at strangers who pass by their house. Intact males may stop every few feet during leashed walks and leave urine droplets to alert other dogs of their presence. Intact females may come in season. Never leave a female in season outside unsupervised. Instead, limit her outdoor time to being on a leash in her own backyard.

Timely Training Tips. Be consistent with your training and socialization techniques, and step up your positive interactions with your nearly grown puppy. Increase the amount of exercise your puppy gets. Aim for two or three walks a day for a minimum of fifteen minutes per session, but adjust this depending on the activity needs of your dog: Some dogs may need an hour of vigorous activity a day. Introduce your dog to an organized sport, such as agility (an obstacle course for dogs) or Frisbee catching, depending on her interest and health status. Beef up your lessons in recall and impulse control during this age.

Be a Teacher, not a Task Master

Duford's title is professional dog trainer, but she really is part psychologist and part cheerleader. She must find ways to motivate both people and their pets seamlessly. She reminds her students that their attitude highly influences how their puppies act and react. Puppies respond to people's emotions even if they don't know what these emotions, such as happiness or frustration, may mean. "When a puppy gets really worked up, really excited, the best way to tone down those emotions is for you to calm yourself," she says. "Puppies read our body cues, our emotions."

"Dogs are obedient to the laws of learning," says Duford. "If you want your dog to do something, find a way for it to make sense to her and she will respond." Basically, puppies, just like people, are more willing to learn when there are good payoffs. They also tend to avoid things that are unpleasant. Puppies live in the moment. If your puppy gets a treat every time she sits, she will be motivated to sit more. But if you come home and yell at her for making puppy puddles, she will learn to avoid this unpleasant experience by not bounding to greet you.

There is no single blueprint that works on all puppies. There is no magic wand to wave that will turn your puppy into Miss Manners.

Duford offers a variety of positive reinforcement training tools so that people can select the ones that best suit their individual puppy's needs. Not all puppies, for instance, are chowhounds—only motivated by food treats. Some will do *anything* to gain the opportunity to chase a tennis ball or snare a Frisbee; others long for praise and petting. Puppies usually learn hand signals quickly but may need more time to learn auditory cues. "Positive reinforcement rewards the puppy for doing something right," explains Duford. "People should view their puppies as learners. We're their teachers. Once people recognize that their puppies are pupils, they have more empathy for and patience with them."

In essence, with positive reinforcement mistakes are ignored and successes—even small ones—are praised.

Teaching the Basics

Out with the word *no* and in with the word *yes*. Accentuate the positive in puppy training. The *yes* can be verbal or conveyed by using a clicker to reinforce a desired behavior (Please see the service dogs chapter for clicker basics.)

"To shape a behavior, you need a way to communicate quickly, and I like to use a clicker or the word *yes*," says Duford. "Start by showing your puppy that the word means something positive. Give a click or, say, "Yes!" and then hand her a treat or a toy. Then repeat until she associates the sound with a reward." Some puppies catch on quickly. Be patient and you will see positive results. And practice timing. For reinforcement to be effective, it should occur during the behavior. Once the pattern of reward is established each time that the puppy does the right action, you can go on a random schedule. This random reinforcement keeps your puppy happily anticipating when she will receive the pay-off—very similar to people playing slot machines in hopes of hitting jackpots.

Break down a new trick or behavior into baby steps and focus on teaching one step at a time. Build on your puppy's progress. And, if you don't succeed during one session, take a break. Try again later rather than insisting that the puppy master this step now. Consistent training and a lot of playful interactions can help your puppy grow into a smart and happy dog. Here are some basic behaviors to show off just how smart your puppy is:

TEACHING *SIT*

Hold a treat in front of your puppy's nose and motion up and back at a 45-degree angle. Your puppy will follow the treat, bending her head back until she sits. Click and treat. Repeat this a few times. Next, show her the treat, but don't lure her with it. Wait until she sits on her own,

Teach sit *by holding a treat in front of your puppy's nose and motioning up and back at a 45-degree angle.*

then click and treat. Repeat this until she immediately sits every time you show her a treat. Now, increase the length of time your puppy stays seated before you click. If she gets up before you click, start over. Once your puppy consistently follows your hand cue, introduce the verbal cue *sit* just before she sits. Click and treat.

If your puppy doesn't sit when you show her the food treat the first time, break the exercise down into smaller components. If you keep your cues consistent, your puppy will be a pro at sitting on cue.

TEACHING *LEAVE IT*

Hold an object in front of you, in the palm of your hand. When your puppy reaches for the object, close your hand and pull away. Repeat this step until your puppy stops reaching for the object. Next, click and, say, "Get it." Increase the length of time your puppy waits to reach for the object before you click.

Now, place the object on the floor. If your puppy reaches for it, cover it with your foot or hand. When your puppy consistently leaves the object alone, add the cue *leave it* just before you present the object. As soon as she backs off, click and, say, "Leave it." Gradually increase the length of time your puppy must leave the object alone. Practice with different objects, and see if you can work up to moving around while your dog leaves it.

TEACHING *DOWN*

Start with your puppy sitting. Hold a treat in front of her nose, and motion with it straight down to the floor between her paws. She most likely will follow the treat to the floor, lying down as she does. As soon as she is lying down, click and treat. Repeat the process, but with each successful repetition, lure less so your puppy learns to lie down without as much help from you. When you lure and she consistently lies down, add your cue, saying, "Down" just before you show her the treat. She will make the connection and lie down when you, say, "Down."

Teach down *by holding a treat in front of your puppy's nose and motioning* down *while your puppy is in the* sit *position.*

As you make learning more challenging, your puppy may take longer to figure out what you want, so be positive and patient. If your puppy doesn't lie down when you lure her, don't worry. You may need to break this behavior down into smaller steps. In time, you won't be able to show her a treat without her throwing herself into a down position to earn a click and a treat.

TEACHING *COME*

Turn training into playtime by using the classic children's game of hide-and-seek to reinforce the *come* cue with your puppy. Practice this game inside your house with the help of a friend or family member. Have someone hold your puppy while you hide in the house. Then call your puppy, saying, "Mollie, Come!" You may need to repeat her name a few times until she reaches you. Click and treat when she does. While you reward your puppy, have your friend hide and call your puppy's name.

This is a fun way to teach the *come* cue, and it also teaches persistence in your puppy's search for you—definitely a good cue to know in case you and your puppy get separated out-doors. Duford recommends using an extra special treat exclusively for teaching *come* to ensure your puppy will respond to this cue. The message you want to convey to your puppy is that when you say *come*, your puppy stops whatever she is doing and comes to you.

Crate Introductions

Puppies need a safe, comfy place to call home, which is what crates provide puppies. Duford recommends introducing crates to puppies in positive, gradual steps. Start by keeping the crate door open and standing by the crate. When your curious puppy approaches and sniffs the crate, click and treat. Build up the attraction of the crate by tossing the treat inside, and work up to shutting the crate door with your puppy inside by giving her a treat and letting her out. Gradually increase your distance from the crate to teach your puppy that she can survive, even if you're out of sight.

By doing these exercises, you're building a positive association for your puppy with the crate. As your puppy learns to love her crate, try crating her in a car for a safe ride—your puppy may view it as her bedroom on wheels.

Leash Walking

Puppies certainly unleash a lot of energy, but they need to rein in some of that enthusiasm. That's where leash training enters the scene. When the leash is slack or when your puppy turns her attention to you, click and treat. Reinforce every step your puppy takes with a slack leash. If she pulls, stop and/or walk backwards until she orients her body to you. As soon as she does, click and treat, and walk forward again.

Soon your puppy will learn that the only way to walk forward is on a slack leash and that pulling means stopping or backing up. Once your puppy catches on to this game, you can simply praise her for walking politely: The reward of continuing the walk reinforces polite walking.

Table Manners

Puppies *love* dinnertime and often become anxious, jumping, panting, and wagging their tail for a meal. But, you can teach your puppy to behave politely when waiting for food. First, ask your puppy to lie down. Then, slowly lower her food dish to the floor. Depending on your dog's behavior, you may need to lower the

bowl just a few inches at first. When she does stay, reward her, and gradually lower the bowl closer to the floor with each repetition. If your puppy leaps up, lift up the dish and wait for her to lie down again. When she does lie down, lower the dish again. When she remains lying until the dish touches the floor, release her and let her eat.

Once your puppy masters this stage, work on having her stay for varying lengths of time when the dish is on the floor, even when you turn your back or exit the room. Teaching your puppy table manners makes mealtimes far less chaotic.

Socialize Your Puppy

Socialization is key in proper puppy parenting, and exposing your puppy to a wide variety of people, dogs, places, and circumstances is an important component. Proper social introductions should be viewed as essential as serving nutritionally balanced meals and booking regular medical checkups with your puppy's veterinarian. Duford recommends that puppies meet between one to two hundred people inside and outside the home by the time they are five months old. It is easier than you think. For instance, sit on a park bench on a Sunday afternoon for thirty minutes. The number of people who walk by or stop to pet your puppy will amaze you. Even if your puppy is comfortable with the people and other pets in your house, exposing her to people, pets, and places outside your home helps ensure her comfort with many types of

situations and people. It also helps shape her personality and hone her attitude.

Closer to home, purposely introduce your puppy to someone who comes to your door on a regular basis, such as meter reader, mail carrier, or parcel deliverer. Have this individual give your puppy a small food treat so that your puppy develops a positive association with this person. Encourage friends and family members familiar to your puppy to occasionally wear disguises so that your puppy is exposed to people wearing hats, sunglasses, beards, and funky outfits. Monitor her reaction, and give her treats so that she pairs a strange new experience with something positive. If she seems a little apprehensive, go slower and give more treats.

During adolescence (six to nine months), you may occasionally see fearful responses—especially in dogs between six months and two years. A young dog may suddenly be wary of something she is used to or of being in a new situation. Be conscious of this, and expose your dog to positive situations to help her overcome her fright. Same advice—be patient, give treats, and break down the new encounter into small steps to build her confidence.

Once your puppy completes her puppy vaccines to bolster her immune system, consider these outings:

- Spend fifteen minutes once a week outside a shopping mall or supermarket with your puppy. These busy places provide the perfect meet-and-greet opportunities for your puppy. She will be exposed to people of all ages, various fashions, and various attitudes.

- Take your puppy to an outdoor café. Sip your favorite beverage while your puppy takes in all the sights, sounds, and smells. Be sure to bring a portable bowl, a plastic bottle of water, and a few tasty treats for your puppy so she doesn't start showing off her begging skills to the couple at the next table.

- Bring your puppy with you on quick errands to pick up dry cleaning or a quick lunch from a fast-food restaurant drive-thru. Never leave your puppy inside a car, especially during hot weather. The heat can kill a puppy within five to ten minutes.

- Host weekly backyard dog parties with a few of your friends and their well-behaved puppy-friendly canines. Select an enclosed yard where you can supervise play. This gives your puppy the opportunity to learn the ropes from adult dogs through play. When selecting your doggy guests, make sure they are similar in size. You might not want your Yorkshire terrier puppy interacting with a bullmastiff.

- Organize neighborhood dog walks by inviting a few owners and their dogs to join you in a friendly on-leash jaunt at least once a week. Determine the length of the walk on your puppy's age and stamina. This activity introduces your puppy to breeds of different sizes and ages and may lead to lifelong canine friendships. You also may develop a network of dog lovers who can help you when you are in need of a dog sitter.

• Enroll your puppy in kindergarten classes that cater to puppies between seven and sixteen weeks of age. In these classes, puppies learn basic behaviors, get used to being handled, and learn how to play in a supervised environment. Classes also help puppies learn impulse control so that no one in class becomes a bully or is bullied. Duford says socialization in these classes should never be forced on a shy puppy. Coax shy puppies with treats or toys, and only pet puppies who readily approach on their own.

Conquering Pesky Puppy Behaviors

Even if you enroll your puppy in a class, teach her some basic behaviors, and engage in structured play, you may still need to contend with common puppy behaviors. Topping the list: house soiling, chewing, and getting into everything. Duford offers the following tactics to correct these pesky puppy behaviors.

HOUSE-TRAINING

It is unrealistic to expect a young puppy to hold her bladder or bowels for eight hours during the day while her owner is at work; therefore, people who work full-time should seriously consider not getting a puppy. But if they do, they should hire someone or rely on responsible friends and family members to walk and play with their puppy a few times during the workday. Young puppies, as mentioned earlier, don't have full control over their bowels and bladder until at least age five or six months. So, an occasional "oopsie" may occur on your floor.

For young puppies, Duford recommends taking them outside immediately when they wake up, right after they eat or drink, or engage in playtime. Puppies need to be on a regular schedule—feeding them at the same time every day and removing their food bowl after a meal and their water bowl an hour or two after their final meal of the day. The younger the puppy, the more bathroom breaks she will need. If you see your puppy circling or sniffing, heed these cues—they usually mean your puppy is ready to eliminate.

If you catch your puppy in the act of making a puddle, resist your first inclination to declare, "Aha! Caught you, you bad, bad puppy!" Instead, scoop your puppy up in your arms and escort her outside where she can finish doing her business. As your puppy gets older, go to the door and call her with a key word or phrase, such as *outside*. Your puppy will get the connection that *outside* means go to the door. This key phrase will stick with her throughout adulthood. When she eliminates outside, shower her with praise and give some treats. Skip punishing tones, and focus on praising your puppy when she does go outside. This sends the message that eliminating outside is pleasant *and* pleasing. "Just like a human baby, a puppy will eliminate whenever she needs to until she is physically able to hold it and when she eventually learns to go outside to eliminate," explains Duford. "It is our responsibility to teach the puppy the right place to go."

A room with an easy-to-clean floor, such as the kitchen, is a good place for your puppy when she can't be supervised.

During house-training, Duford tells owners to pick up Persian rugs or any prized rug they don't want dampened by their puppies. When you can't supervise a puppy in house-training, confine her to one room, such as a kitchen with easy-to-clean floors, or a crate as a place of comfort.

If you must work during the day, let your puppy soil on thick layers of newspaper in the corner of a puppy-proofed room or extra large crate. Be patient—just like human babies, some puppies learn proper bathroom habits more quickly than others. If your puppy makes a mess inside, clean it without making a fuss. Try commercial products especially made for pet odors or a homemade mixture of white vinegar and water (half vinegar and half water) to deodorize the urine smell.

CHEWING AND NIPPING

Puppies are very oral. They love exploring their new surroundings by sticking new objects in their mouth, including your hand and the arm of the couch. Chewing is also a natural way for puppies to ease the pain of tender gums caused by the replacement of baby teeth with adult teeth. Accept the fact that your puppy will chew and that teething is perfectly normal for puppies up to twelve

weeks, or even longer. But, also recognize that you can control what she chews. Direct her away from your favorite leather shoes, electrical cords, and your fingers by offering her acceptable chew objects, such as hard rubber toys, sterilized bones, Nylabones, and Kong toys. Stuff hollow bones and Kongs with peanut butter or cream cheese to make them more desirable. Avoid tossing your puppy an old shoe—she won't be able to distinguish that smelly old reject from your brand-new black leather heels.

When your puppy bites your hand, forearm, pant leg, or anywhere on you, let out a surprised, "OUCH!" or a high-pitched squeal to

let your puppy know that she bit too hard. Puppies must learn about bite inhibition—unfortunately, this skill is not built into their genetic code. Bite inhibition teaches your puppy to control the pressure of her mouth and her jaws, preventing you or someone else any harm. If your puppy persists despite your "Ouch!" turn to stage two: Stop petting or playing with her. Give her the cold shoulder treatment, turning your back and ignoring her for thirty seconds or more. She will learn, *When I put my mouth on you, no more nice stuff comes my way.*

Duford also uses counterconditioning to stop puppies from being mouthy. By taking things that normally trigger mouthing—petting or playing—implementing them at low intensity levels, and pairing them with treats, you are essentially changing the association of petting and mouthing to petting and a treat. For example, touching your puppy, then giving her a treat or trimming a nail, then giving her a treat.

NOSY NELLIE

Puppies are naturally investigative—they need to sniff and check out everything. A little housekeeping can take away many temptations and save your household items—and your sanity.

For starters, says Duford, keep toilet lids down and bathroom doors shut. Keep socks and other clothing items in dresser drawers or in closets with doors. Store household cleaners on high shelves or inside cabinets with childproof plastic locks. Pick up loose change, earrings, and other small items that can be swallowed. Tuck away electrical cords and spray them with Bitter Apple to discourage chewing. Hoist plants on ceiling hooks or place them on high sturdy shelves or counters. Use child gates in open doorways, or place your puppy in a crate so that she can view activities around her but still be in a safe area.

Puppy parenting can be challenging, says Duford. Training begins the day you bring home your puppy and should continue throughout her life. "Training is really about everyday interaction, so be consistent and provide positive outlets for your puppy's energy," says Duford. "And, understand that learning is not a straight progression. Puppies have good days and bad days, just like people."

JOCK DOGS AND THE SPORTING LIFE

Profiled Trainer: Susan Garrett

The doorbell rings at the Garrett home in Hamilton, Ontario. On cue, eight Garrett children try to suppress giggles and keep silent upstairs as their parents and older sister, Vicki, politely greet the professional dog breeder delivering their new poodle puppy. "The breeder didn't want to sell the puppy to a big family," recalls Susan Garrett, who was five at the time the family adopted Tina the poodle. "My parents instructed us to stay upstairs and not make a sound. But Tina proved to be a great dog who could handle a big family."

Susan, the seventh youngest among the siblings, taught the ever-attentive Tina how to perform *roll over*, *play dead*, *sit*, and *stay* commands. Tina

"The more frequently a desired behavior is reinforced, the more frequently a dog will repeat it in hopes of further reinforcement." — SUSAN GARRETT

was also taught to obey household boundaries, making sure she steered clear of the dining room and living room.

While Susan's father, Victor, worked in the steel mills and spent his off-hours helping Susan's mother, Rita, buy, fix-up, and sell houses, Susan spent her free time with her sister, Vicki, at dog confirmation shows. "I guess you could say that my sister is probably why I got interested in dogs and training," says Susan. "She would show Irish wolfhounds, and I spent a lot of time watching and learning." Susan broadened her interest to horses during her high school and college years, learning how to train horses and compete in dressage events. "I learned that you need a good partnership between you and the animal," she says. "I also learned never to move too fast."

She seemed headed toward a career as a veterinarian when she enrolled at the University of Guelph until she discovered that she was allergic to all animals but horses. The itchy eyes, runny nose, and throat-closing symptoms surfaced when she was milking cows and teaching basic obedience commands to puppies on a farm to earn spending money. Determined to enter an animal-related field, she changed her major and earned a degree in animal science. After enduring four needle injections a week for four years, Susan developed a tolerance for dogs but "still can't go into a cattle barn without having a reaction."

In the late eighties, Susan adopted Shelby, a Jack Russell terrier puppy. When Shelby was twelve weeks old, Susan enrolled her in a dog training school. Within a year, the instructors invited her to teach classes because of her natural ability to bring out the best in dogs. At the same time, she and Shelby competed—and earned top prizes—in agility and flyball events, including national championships in the United States Dog Agility Association (USDAA) and the North American Dog Agility Council (NADAC) organizations. "Shelby is just a hoot," describes Susan. "I've discovered that her number one training tool is an ordinary rock—I give her a rock at ring side a lot."

In addition to Shelby, Susan's canine athletic squad includes:

- **Stoni:** This eleven-year-old Border collie is Susan's "gift from God." There has never been a dog born like her. She has been the best at whatever she tries, and at age ten, was on a flyball team that set a yet-to-be-beat international record of 16.06 seconds. She won multiple national championships in agility and was the Pedigree Canada Obedience Dog of the Year in 1996. "She's athletic, fast, and very, very clever."

- **Twister:** This eight-year-old Jack Russell terrier is blessed with blazing speed and a big-dog-in-a-little-dog's-body attitude. She won NADAC and United States Dog Agility Association (USDAA) national champi-onships in agility and showed off her ability to "pray" in a comedy starring members of the *Saturday Night Live* cast. She is also Susan's "little soul mate" because of her

compassion. When Susan learned that her mother, Rita, was diagnosed with stomach cancer, Twister stayed by her side. "My mom and I were very close, and when I would spend time with my mom before she died, it helped that Twister was there with me," says Susan.

- **Buzz:** Just like the jolt one gets from drinking too much caffeine, this five-year-old Border collie earns his name due to his hyperactive personality. "In agility competitions, he barks his whole way around the course and loves to announce his exuberance," says Susan. "But, he could be the poster canine for clicker training. He gives positive rein-forcement training programs credibility because he can be such a challenging dog." Buzz is also a national agility champion in USDAA and Agility Association of Canada (AAC).

- **Decaff:** This one-year-old Jack Russell terrier is a driven dog who not only loves to work but also enjoys cuddling with Susan. "Definitely, a momma's girl," describes Susan. "Decaff is in training for flyball and agility, and I take her with me at seminars and use her for puppy training demonstrations."

- **Quid:** Named after British money, this two-year-old Border collie is another dog in performance training. Susan's life partner, John Blenkey, is the owner and trainer of Quid.

"All of these dogs are our pets and members of our family," declares Susan, who shares a home on 28 acres with John, an obedience judge in Alberton, Ontario. "Each night, they sleep in the bedroom with John and I, but each dog has his or her own bed."

Until 2000, Susan juggled a full-time, demanding job in veterinary pharmaceutical sales while teaching dog training classes and competing. She lived, it seemed, out of a suitcase. "I kept getting invited to speak at different dog workshops and conferences and would leave on a Friday afternoon from my sales job, spend the entire weekend teaching, and return on a red-eye flight early Monday morning and go directly back to work," says Susan. "It was an exhausting schedule."

Now, she is finally able to devote her full attention to training dogs and their owners in a variety of performance canine sports—with the emphasis always on fun. She successfully teaches people how to use clicker training for obedience, agility, flyball, and trick training. "I never use force in my training methods," she says. "Dogs simply learn the best by recognizing the consequences of their behavior. When they do the right action, they get rewarded; when they don't, they get no rewards. In time, you notice how the dog's behavior gets shaped, so innately he starts choosing the action you want him to do."

Introduction

In the world of competitive agility, Garrett's dogs are consistently at the top. Her pair of Jack Russell terriers, Shelby and Twister, and her Border collies Stoni and Buzz have reigned as national agility champs. Stoni and Twister also run on the world-record-setting flyball team. But more importantly, all of her dogs are physically fit, full of fun, and totally in tune with Garrett.

Fortunately, Garrett also excels at teaching performance sports to people and their dogs. Although she calls Alberton, Ontario, home, she travels throughout Canada, the United States, Japan, England, and other countries to

A-frame

present her on-target, down-to-earth coaching style at training conferences. Her goal is to have all dogs and handlers ultimately walk away as better teammates with a greater understanding of each other.

The payoffs for training in agility, Frisbee, canine musical freestyle, flyball, and other canine performance sports goes far beyond the chance for blue ribbons, shiny trophies, or titles, reminds Garrett. By introducing your dog to structured play, both of you reap benefits: Your friendship bond will strengthen as you learn to work as a harmonious team, and the calorie-burning activities will help you both tone your muscles and improve your stamina. Sports serve as a healthy outlet for dogs to use their minds and muscles, reducing the incidence of behavioral problems sparked by boredom or

Dog walk

Start your weave-pole training with the weave poles at least shoulder width apart, and gradually narrow the poles until they are in a straight line.

inactivity. And, athleticism requires more than pure physical prowess: It also depends on mental focus. That's why Garrett relies on operant conditioning to teach her training concepts. She believes a dog learns through the consequences of his behaviors and actions. When a dog does what an owner wants, he gets praised and rewarded. When a dog does something that displeases an owner, such as bolting outside before having a leash put on his collar, he is called back so he doesn't get the reward of being outside. "The more frequently a desired behavior is reinforced, the more frequently a dog will repeat it in hopes of further reinforcement," adds Garrett.

When it comes to performance sports, the more motivators you have to reward your dog with the better. Some dogs prefer to work for food, but it is up to you as the trainer to expose them to other rewards. Keep your training sessions short and upbeat with a high rate of reinforcement, says Garrett. Be careful

Seesaw

Hurdle

to not let your dog get worried while working. A happy-to-learn dog will pay you back by responding to you as his trainer in a very upbeat fashion.

An Inside Look at Agility

Agility is a fast-growing sport that requires a person to guide a dog over a timed course, featuring several obstacles. Dogs must race against the clock as they scale ramps, bulldoze through tunnels, leap over hurdles, traverse a seesaw, and snake in and out of a line of weave poles. Scoring is based on how cleanly and quickly the dog performs in specific classes, based on ability and size. During competition, people race along side their dogs but are not

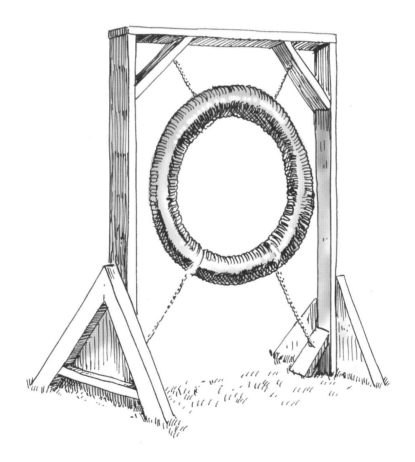

Hoop jump

allowed to physically touch their dogs. They must rely on hand signals and verbal commands to guide their dogs through the various obstacles in an order predetermined by an agility judge. Dogs lose points for failing to put one or more feet on designated contact zones, knocking over hurdles, taking obstacles out of order, skipping obstacles, or not completing the course in a set time limit. Typical obstacles in an agility course include: A-frame, seesaw, dog walk, tunnels (pipe and collapsed), weave poles, tire or hoop jump, hurdles, and a pause table.

Once the domain of Border collies and shelties, agility now attracts dogs of all shapes, sizes, and breeds, from surprisingly quick-turning Pomeranians to power-pushing keeshonds. Garrett encourages owners to maximize the best their dogs have to offer. Age, weight, physical stature, and breed play key roles in how well your dog will master leaping over hurdles, scaling up and down A-frames, and bulleting through mounted tires.

Special Health Considerations

Before you rush into the agility ring or sign your dog up for the next local flyball event, pull back a little on your enthusiasm. You may think you own an athletic dog but remember, even the top jock dogs are far from being invincible. Just like us, canine athletes can suffer injuries due to improper or inadequate training. Before introducing your dog to any performance sport, Garrett recommends booking an appointment with your veterinarian so that your dog can receive a thorough physical exam. Your veterinarian may discover that your dog has some limiting physical condition, such as hip or elbow dysplasia, or may need to lose a few extra pounds before attempting the rigors of an agility obstacle course.

If your dog is a bit chubby, gradually extend the time you spend on your daily walks and step up the pace. Also, replace fatty table scraps with healthier treats, such as raw carrots. Aim for a 5 percent weight loss per week to ensure that the excess pounds come off steadily and stay off.

Avoid introducing your growing puppy to sports too soon. Growth plates in dogs do not fully form until twelve to eighteen months, depending on the breed. In agility, for

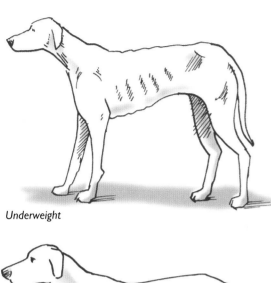

Underweight

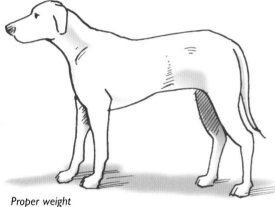

Proper weight

Overweight

instance, young dogs should jump hurdles only a few inches high, until they reach physical maturity, to reduce the risk of bone breaks and muscle tears.

Sidestep the weekend warrior mentality by resisting the temptation to turn your dog into a Saturday-Sunday jock from a weekday sofa lounger. Dogs who are not consistently exercised run the risk of pulling muscles or lack the stamina to complete an agility course. During the week, incorporate short sprints during your daily walks to build stamina for both of you. If your dog likes water, try swimming together to improve your cardiovascular condition and to tone muscles.

Prior to any physical activity with your dog, devote five to ten minutes stretching you and your dog's muscles to warm them. Garrett recommends that you have your dog get into a play bow position (front paws stretched out front, head down, and back end up) and maintain that stretch for five to ten seconds. Then, place your dog on his side and gently but firmly stretch each of his legs, one at a time. Hold each leg stretch for five seconds before releasing. Then have your dog take a few practice jumps over hurdles.

To help prevent injury before an activity, get your dog in the play bow position to stretch his muscles.

As you begin to train together, set realistic goals that mirror your dog's abilities and interest. Don't let your decisions be ruled by your personal ego-defined desires. Sure, it would be great to own the world's top agility dog, but at what price? Focus on teaching your dog at his pace so you are successful along the way.

Don't Overlook Obedience

Before a canine athlete can clear a hurdle, snag a Frisbee in midair, or dance the cha-cha in time to music, he must master basic obedience commands. He should be able to *sit*, *stay*, and *lie down* on command, and, most importantly, come when called by his owner. "You need to feel confident that your dog will come to you each and every time you call him by name, no matter where you are or what the distractions may be," says Garrett.

She offers this step-by-step guide to strengthen the recall response in your dog:

- Identify distractions—people, toys, food, smells, places, and situations that your dog finds distracting to the point of not paying attention to you.

- Rate these distractions on a scale of one to ten with ten being the most distractive.

- Spend a week desensitizing your dog from these distractions. Keep him on a leash whenever there are any distractions you rate a two or higher.

- Do not expose your dog to distractions rated a ten for two months, whenever possible. Doing so eliminates your dog's choice in deciding whether to come to you when a ten distraction is present.

- Devote three, five-minute sessions each day to practicing recall commands with your dog. Aim for fifteen to twenty-five recalls during each session in a quiet place with no distractions.

- Select different motivators to reward your dog each time he comes to you on command. Use toys or different types of foods that your dog especially prizes. Choose a specific phrase, such as *come to me*, not just the generalized *come* command each time.

- Gradually add a few distractions that rate a one on your scale and call for your dog. You need to execute at least twenty successful recalls before progressing to the next step.

- Do not say your dog's name before the *come to me* cue when playing the recall game. In two months or so your dog will fully understand that adding the mention of his name to the *come to me* cue will be a bonus.

- Progress up your distraction chart as your dog demonstrates that he will *come* on cue. By the end of eight weeks, you should have tallied about twenty recalls per training session, three times a day for a grand total of 3,360 successful recalls with your dog. This gives you a solid foundation for shaping your dogs behavior. Now, every time you, say, "Murphy, come to me," he will sprint to you no matter what distractions or temptations are present.

Agility Training

STAYING FOCUSED

Garrett coined the acronym DASH to help her students stay focused during their training sessions. Simply, DASH stands for:

Desire. Before you try to teach your dog any trick, you need to display your excitement and enthusiasm. Your upbeat attitude should be read—and adopted—by your dog. If necessary, motivate your dog with a fun activity, such as a quick game of tug, before you begin your training sessions to get him ready to focus on you.

Accuracy. Once your dog is motivated to learn, you can start shaping the accuracy of a specific behavior or agility skill.

Speed. Once your dog has mastered a skill or sequence of skills, you're ready to work on ways to trim seconds off the time it takes your dog to perform these skills.

Habitat. You need to practice agility with your dog in different settings—beyond your backyard or indoor agility class. Exposing your dog to different locations helps him associate agility skills to different places, especially inside the competition ring.

"Most importantly, never proceed forward until you are absolutely thrilled with the attitude, intensity, desire, and overall performance of your dog," says Garrett.

FIVE IMPORTANT ASPECTS OF AGILITY

Garrett shares her inside training secrets to five important aspects of agility: introducing a new motivator, adding speed, mastering weave poles, contact obstacles, and staying on course.

Turning a Ho-Hum into a Hooray. Some people proudly declare that their dog will do *anything* to play with his Frisbee or favorite squeaky toy. Encouraging a dog to love only one particular toy can actually be a drawback to performance sports training, says Garrett. "The dog becomes focused entirely on the reward—the favorite toy—and not the game that you are trying to play with him," says Garrett. "They perform agility just for what they may get when it is over rather than playing because they enjoy the game."

Her solution: Introduce your dog to a variety of objects that initially garner only a yawn in interest and slowly build their value. Start

by working with a toy your dog deems to have little or no value. One of Garrett's favorite choices is a tennis ball-on-a-rope toy. Cut a slit in the ball about 1 1/2 inch long and load small pieces of kibble or other treats to enhance the value of the toy. Elevate the status of the toy in the eyes of your dog by pairing it up with cues your dog gets excited over. For example, if your dog leaps into the air with delight each time you grab your car keys, start picking up the tennis ball toy first before you pick up the car keys. Or, place the toy on the counter before you bring out his food bowl. Prepare his food but place the toy where you normally place his food bowl. Wait a few minutes and then put the bowl down next to the toy. The light bulb will soon click on inside your dog's head as he starts to realize that the presence of the toy signals something wonderful is about to happen.

You are now ready to shape your dog's ability to retrieve the toy. Kneel at your dog's eye level and let him watch you plop a few small pieces of treats into the slit of the ball. Toss the ball in front of your dog. As soon as he looks at the ball, hit your clicker or, say, "Yes." Go over to the ball, pick it up, and shake out a treat for your dog. Repeat this a few times before storing the toy in a drawer. (Please see the service dogs chapter for clicker basics.)

During the next session, toss the toy but click only when your dog walks toward the ball. Gradually raise your criteria so that your dog receives treats only when he touches or picks up the ball. During this time, do not speak any words of encouragement. In time, your dog will gain confidence to pick up the toy and march it to you before you click and treat. What you are doing is teaching your dog a new interactive way to have fun with you. That thinking should carry over to the agility course.

Bring on the Speed. Does your dog conquer each obstacle cleanly in an agility course but seem to take his own sweet time? Without meaning to offend, Garrett says dogs are often slow because owners unintentionally communicate for them to follow that tempo. In your quest to figure out how to teach your dog to pick up speed and still maintain his accuracy, you may overlook the cause behind the slowdown, which is actually you, not your dog.

"Perhaps your dog was a little nervous when he crept across the dog walk and you assure him with soothing words like, 'That's okay Freddie, you can do it,' " says Garrett. "The words have no meaning to your dog, but your tone does. He recognizes it as a tone of praise and may interpret your desires as, *Okay, so Mama likes it when I go SLOW. I can do that!* Or, maybe you fished out a treat from your pocket to lure your dog to finish walking the plank. Your dog interprets this action to mean, *When I hesitate and stop, Mama feeds me. I can do that, too!* Without realizing it, you have reinforced inappropriate, s-l-o-w behavior."

The Ins and Outs of Weave Poles. In fine-tuning or shaping a dog's ability to wiggle in and out of the weave poles, Garrett rates the clicker as an essential training tool. A clicker helps convey to a dog that he did a particular part of the activity correctly and is the only training aid that you should use to pull your dog out of the poles. Remember to reward only the part of the performance you want a round of applause for and that timing is crucial.

When introducing the challenge of weave poles to your dog, start with a very small set, two for example, suggests Garrett. When your dog will race through those, you can add one or two more poles for him to weave through. The sound of the click isolates which part of the behavior you want to reward. If you click only when your dog completely finishes the weave poles, he may think he was supposed to slow down and wait for the sound of the click to confirm he performed correctly. Select one part of the weave poles to focus on. If your dog finds the correct entry, click and then go to the dog, reward him, and pull him out of the poles to start again. The next time through, select a different part of the weave poles to reward. By isolating small steps of the weaving performance, you strengthen your dog's overall mastery of this obstacle, says Garrett. You will help build your dog's confidence so that he can soon race through a set of twelve weave poles at an event, at top speed.

Contact Obstacles. In certain obstacles in agility, a dog must step on a yellow painted stripe—known as a contact—in order to stay penalty-free during the competition. Dogs must be trained not to leap over these stripes. Contact obstacles, such as the dog walk or A-frame, are often the toughest for dogs to master. One of the best ways to teach your dog to maneuver across an angled contact obstacle is to use a flight of stairs at home. This gives you a safe environment that is free from distraction.

First, use your clicker to train your dog to touch his nose to a clear plastic target. (Please see the service dogs chapter for further explanation.) Place the target at the base of the stairs. Starting at the first step above the base of the stairs, let your dog come down the step,

The correct way for your dog to enter the weave poles is from right to left, with the farthest pole on his right.

directing him to the target. Your dog will learn to move down the step toward the target to touch his nose.

Once he has mastered coming down one step, move him back to the second step. Work up to fading the target so that your dog moves down one or two stairs and lowers his nose to the ground without the target. Keep moving up the stairs until he can race down a flight of stairs and lower his nose to the ground. You want your dog to stay in this position until you release him from the stairs.

Once your dog has learned how much fun it is to race down the stairs to a target position, you can transfer this behavior to a lowered A-frame or dog walk outdoors.

Stay on Course. Have your dog run through the course and touch the specific targets with his nose. Click and then offer a food or toy reward. Repeat this a couple times. Then move the target out and start clicking before your dog reaches the target. What you are doing is reinforcing your dog to go through the pylons (a post or tower marking a prescribed course). Remove the target so that now your dog is run-

Stairs provide a good at-home training tool for contact obstacles.

ning through the pylons. Associate this action with a cue, such as *go, go, go*.

During competition, never take your eyes off your dog. Maintain focus, says Garrett. Always tell your dog where to go before you tell him what you want him to do. Don't unload your frustration on your dog and even after a subpar performance, always praise your dog and reward him as soon as he exits the ring. After all, you enter this sport to have fun and spend quality time with your dog. If you display a win-at-all-costs attitude, your dog will lose his zest to participate. When it comes to agility or any other dog performance sport, Garrett reminds owners to never underestimate the fun factor in learning. If you keep the training fun, upbeat, and positive, your dog will leap at the chance to master another skill.

HELPFUL HOMEWORK HINTS

Garrett encourages people to enroll in performance sports training classes but reminds them that learning does not end when class is over. The best students practice at home what they learn in the classroom. She shares these training tips and concepts to hone your skills when you're at home with your dog:

- **Positive does not equal permissive.** Always be consistent with your dog. Do not allow unwanted behaviors to occur one day and then express your displeasure when your dog does the very same behavior the next day. Your dog depends on your guidance, so be clear and consistent on what behaviors are acceptable.

- **Videotape one training session every other week.** Taping will help you document your progress with your dog. Use these videotapes to determine how well you are performing as a teacher to your dog.

- **Plan your work and work your plan.** Think of yourself as a teacher mapping out lesson plans for your dog. Bring a timer with you or count reinforcements so you don't train your dog to exhaustion. Keep your training sessions short—under ten minutes. Jot down your progress and future lesson plans in a journal.

- **Vary your reinforcement enticements.** Use favorite toys and foods as rewards. Use food to reinforce an attempt to play, but never use food to reinforce a dog that has declined the chance to play.

- **Remind yourself that you are responsible for any shortcomings.** Mistakes? Blame yourself, not your dog. Your dog is strictly a mirror image of your abilities as a trainer. Accept any miscues and work on them.

- **Know what you are reinforcing when you hand out a reward.** If your dog jumps on you after each click and you give him a tasty treat, you are reinforcing his jumping on you, not the intended behavior, such as his recall response. You need to deliver rewards within one second of clicking to reinforce the skill you desire.

- **Practice, practice, practice.** Professional athletes need to train and work on their skills. So should you. Train to improve your weaknesses so that you and your dog become proficient in all aspects of the performance sport.

- **Beware of boredom.** Attitude is everything. If you speak in a monotone voice and use very little gestures, your dog will soon regard agility as a chore or a big bore. Get animated and praise, praise, praise. Let your dog see that you're having a grand time.

- **Set the rules of the game.** Choose which toy your dog will play with when the game starts and when the game ends.

- **Slow down.** You can't have speed without understanding. Make sure that your dog can accurately perform a specific skill before you try to speed him up.

- **Know when to call it quits.** Always end your daily training before your dog becomes physically or mentally exhausted.

★ ★ ★ ★ ★ ★ ★ ★ ★

SERVICE DOGS: WHEN YOU NEED AN EXTRA SET OF "HANDS"

★ ★ ★ ★ ★ ★ ★ ★ ★

Profiled Trainer: Debi Davis

Reflecting on her childhood, Debi Davis now believes she was raised clicker-style by her forever-positive parents. Of course, back then the term hadn't been coined and her parents weren't exactly pressing a noise-making device each time that Debi and her siblings made the right move. But her parents had a knack for redirecting their three children toward more appropriate behaviors without raising their voices. "None of us children were spanked or hollered at once," says Debi, age fifty-three, who grew up as the youngest on a 10-acre property outside the city limits of Romulus, Michigan, a Detroit suburb. "My dad was very creative and open minded. My mom found operant ways to change our behaviors so as not to stress us or belittle us but to build on our strengths. She was incredibly patient and always found ways to make chores we didn't want to do into fun games."

"Dogs like to have jobs, and they like getting attention and interacting with their owners." — DEBI DAVIS

The Davis family abided by certain household rules. "We were never allowed to say something bad about someone in the house—we had to step outside to do so," recalls Debi. "We were also taught to honor the food and the person who made the food. We couldn't say, 'I don't like broccoli or spinach.' Instead, we were taught to take a little bite, swallow it, politely decline any more and say, 'But I will have more potatoes, please.' "

Debi's parents, Steve and Bernice Davis, owned and operated the Davis Collision Service, a place where dented cars came to be restored. In her teens, Debi pitched in, cleaning the cars and detailing them with stripes. She quickly realized that she had not inherited any mechanical skills. But she had shared her entire childhood with animals. She was riding ponies without wobbling by the time she could stand up. Cats and dogs ran in and out of her home day and night, and tadpoles and fish kept Debi's attention each time she went to explore

nearby ponds. So, after graduating from high school, Debi followed her desire to explore by working in various jobs and places. She worked as a dental assistant, she helped to build log cabins in San Francisco and Anchorage, and finally returned to her innate love: animals.

She was working at an Arabian horse breeding farm in South Bend, Indiana, when she first experienced occasional numbness in her legs. Without warning, her foot would become numb; she'd take a step and take a tumble. "Doctors told me that I had a vascular progressive disease but couldn't and still can't find the cause," says Debi. In the past twenty-five years, Debi has undergone thirty-five operations. Her right leg was amputated below the knee in 1977, followed by her left leg being amputated above the knee in 1980. Then the disease began targeting her heart, triggering several heart attacks.

Eight years ago, doctors diagnosed Debi's

condition as terminal, telling her she had only a few months left to live. During this time, she met Tim, a high school math teacher in Tucson, Arizona, who simply adored her and admired her survival spirit. "He asked me to marry him, but I said, 'I can't. I'm dying,' " says Debi. "He persisted, arguing that 'If you don't have long to live, we'd better not have a long engagement, but get married right away so we don't miss a moment of time together.' I said yes and we've been married nearly seven years, and Tim's now my assistant service-dog trainer. I am happy and grateful for each new day."

Using a wheelchair to get around, Debi realized that she needed a dog to help her with daily activities but felt she could no longer adequately exercise a larger dog with her changing health status. She wanted a small dog with a big dog spirit. "I picked Peekaboo, a papillon, because this breed is the closest dog personality-wise to the Border collie," notes Debi. "Like Border collies, papillons are fast learners and quick-moving, yet small enough for me to exercise indoors, when needed. Also, papillons have been bred for centuries to be human companions, ideally suited for animal-assisted therapy work."

But Peekaboo (nicknamed Peek) came to Debi as a three-month-old problem child. He didn't know how to communicate with his own species, except by posturing, growling, and lunging. He also had the same fear-based actions toward human strangers as well as cats, squirrels, and other fast-moving small animals. These small animals caused him to become overly aggressive and not listen to Debi. "He was never socialized with other dogs during puppy hood and would backpedal any time an approaching dog went into a play bow posture to signal, *Hey, it's play time*," says Debi. "Peekaboo also didn't know how to cope with people, especially strangers."

So, Debi and her mother started taking Peekaboo to parks and grocery store entrances to meet and greet people. Not knowing another option, Debi squirted Peekaboo with water from a bottle or gave a leash correction every time he misbehaved. But correcting him during these times proved disastrous: Peek became more aggressive, barked louder, and began snapping at Debi's friends and family members. "The more aggressive I got toward suppressing his bad behavior, the more aggressive and fearful he got," she says. "I only knew traditional training that called for corrections and then praise, but it wasn't working on Peekaboo. The more I punished, the worse Peek became," she continued. "I had no idea what to do, and well-meaning friends began to advise me to consider euthanizing him because he was so out of control. Each daily walk had become a war of wills in which I'd try to force compliance as a tough boss."

Then, Debi read *Don't Shoot the Dog* by internationally acclaimed dog trainer Karen Pryor, and the words inspired her to try positive reinforcement techniques on Peekaboo, and incorporate clicker training into training sessions. Debi moved across the country and enrolled Peek in Handi-Dogs, a service-dog training center teaching people with disabilities how to train their own service dogs. This school uses only clicker training, and no physical or verbal punishment is allowed. It was life-changing for both Peek and Debi.

"When I would 'catch' Peekaboo doing something right, I would praise him and slowly build on his successes," says Debi. "I learned to ignore and redirect unwanted behaviors and to catch my dog doing it right. Now, at age seven, he is a totally different dog—and a much happier one."

And, he's a bit of a canine celebrity, too. In 1999, Peekaboo earned Beyond Limits National Service Dog of the Year honors by the Delta Society, the national organization dedicated to promoting human health through service and therapy animals based in Renton, Washington. Peekaboo became the first toy breed—and the first clicker-trained dog—to win this prestigious honor usually given to larger, traditional service dogs such as German shepherds or Labrador retrievers.

Debi continues to beat the odds, too. With her medical condition stabilized, she uses her humor, love, and compassion as a professional trainer to teach the benefits of service dogs at conferences, hospitals, nursing homes, and schools. Naturally, Peekaboo comes, too, showing off his ability to pick up a dime on a sidewalk, switch off lights, and fetch a phone. "Peekaboo is my maid, butler, secretary, doorman, sidekick, and, most of all, my best friend," says Debi.

Peekaboo is nearing retirement from his service dog duties due to vision difficulties, and Debi is busy training his successor, Cappy, a three-year-old papillon whose full name is Nitewings Captains Courageous. "Cappy is what I like to call 'bombproof'—nothing bothers him," says Debi. "He was very well socialized as a puppy by his breeder, and he is a natural in our service-dog training classes. You can handle his toes, manipulate his mouth, rub his belly, and make sharp, loud noises and he stays focused on me."

Reflecting on her life, Debi realizes that she has come full circle, carrying on the family tradition of positive guidance to both people and pets. Debi now mentors service-dog teams-in-training around the world, via the Internet, and also helps owners understand how to use clicker-training principles in dealing with human conflicts.

"I feel blessed to have had parents like mine growing up," she says. "I feel so blessed to have had parents who understood the power of positive reinforcement. And now I'm raising my animals in the same manner. It seems so natural to me."

Introduction

The alarm clock sounds at seven o'clock in the morning in Davis's bedroom. Peekaboo knows to silence the alarm with a well-placed paw to the off button. He nudges Davis. She yawns, stretches, and gives Peek a couple minutes of cuddling. She inches to the edge of the bed and gets into her wheelchair.

When it's time for Davis to make her bed, Peekaboo jumps into position on the far side of the mattress. "Tug the covers," Davis instructs Peekaboo. Grasping the sheet between his tiny teeth, he hoists it toward the top of the bed and then uses his teeth to pull the comforter up into place. "I dream of ways to teach him to pour me a cup of coffee or drive the car, but so far those training techniques have eluded me," says Davis with a laugh. "I don't know what I'd do without him." From morning to night, Peekaboo assists her. He fetches the television remote, tugs clothes out of the dryer, picks up dropped pencils, and opens doors on cue.

Most service dogs are large breeds such as golden retrievers or German shepherds, but Peekaboo proves that small dogs can also assist people with physical impairments or psychological conditions, such as panic disorders or agoraphobia (fear of leaving the home to avoid open or public places). Large dogs are better suited to pull wheelchairs, open heavy doors, and provide brace and balance for people. Small dogs can easily jump from lap to laundry duty, travel easier because of their small size, and may be better choices for people who need help with fine motor skills, such as picking up dropped objects.

"Dogs like to have jobs, and they like getting attention and interacting with their owners," says Davis. "Let's say you do not have a physical disability. Wouldn't it be nice if you could train your dog to pick up your dropped keys on cue if you're coming in the house with an armful of groceries?"

Praise Successes, Ignore Mistakes

Davis takes a correction-free approach to training, which she refers to as errorless learning. She relies on clicker training to teach dogs how to master vital skills and do them with gusto and accuracy. Often, a disabled handler lacks the strength or coordination to physically move a dog or pop the leash to gain the dog's atten-

tion, let alone maintaining a dog's high skill level, which can prove daunting.

"Clicker training allows people with disabilities to train their dogs in a totally hands-off way," explains Davis. "I try to find creative ways to show dogs how to do a task right without resorting to physical punishment. The only 'punishment' is what is called negative punishment. For example, good things, such as praise and attention, end when a dog jumps on you. I simply turn my back until the dog calms down and sits. Dogs quickly learn that good things happen when they do something right and stop when they do something wrong."

Davis is a big fan of clicker training because the technique sets a dog up for success, offering positive reinforcement and reward without stress. Clicker training allows mistakes to be part of the normal learning process. Errors are ignored and successes are recognized and rewarded. "Clicker training gives us a way to get information to a dog in a neutral, nonthreatening way," explains Davis. "When a dog realizes she will not be punished for making mistakes, she becomes an active problem-solving participant in training, and learning becomes a dance of joy instead of a stressful journey."

Clicker Basics

Clicker training is a training method that breaks down exercises or behaviors for dogs into small increments and rewards them with a clicking noise a handler makes from squeezing a palm-sized clicker each time a dog performs correctly. The method is first used with a primary reinforcer (something your puppy strongly desires, such as food or attention), then with a conditioned reinforcer, the clicker (a device that initially makes a meaningless sound until it is associated with the primary reinforcer). When the two are linked they form a gentle, effective communication-based method of training.

To teach your dog that the sound of a click precedes something good, Davis recommends that owners click and toss a small food treat to their dogs. The treat should be small and soft so that the food can be quickly ingested. Click and treat several times in a row and watch your dog begin to anticipate the click sound.

Congratulations! You've just mastered the first important step in clicker training. Follow this up with an attention cue by saying your dog's name. Each time your dog makes eye contact with you, click and then provide a small treat. Do this inside and outside with increasingly more distractions. This offers safety benefits because you have trained your dog to associate the sound of his name with a positive reward, which will come in handy if your dog slips off his leash.

The secret to clicker training is timing: The clicker sound must happen at the exact moment that your dog offers the desired behavior. "Clicker training removes the fuzzy edges of learning for a dog," explains Davis. "It tells her exactly when she's got it right, eliminating confusion for the dog."

Once your dog demonstrates proficiency, you're ready to move into the second phase known as variable reinforcement (gradually asking for multiple behaviors before clicking and providing treats for only the very best attempts). This technique operates much like slot machines: You keep pouring in the quarters hoping the next time you pull the lever, you will receive a big payoff; your dog keeps per-

forming the desired behavior in hope of getting a reward.

When training your dog, Davis recommends limiting training sessions to three to five minutes and conducting them periodically throughout the day so that learning becomes part of your dog's normal daily routine.

Target Training

The core behavior behind many successful assistance tasks is what Davis calls target training. The goal is to teach your dog to touch an object with her nose or paw. Once she learns this basic skill, she can close doors, ring doorbells, and push elevator buttons. Target training is more efficient than having to lure directly with food because it does not require food to be present as a bribe. The dog quickly learns to follow the target instead of the food and that working for the click means food or other rewards will follow. "Service dogs are not allowed to sniff the floor or eat food found on restaurant floors or sidewalks, so I use the target stick for teaching many behaviors and to keep the dog's focus off the food all during training. Targeting allows the owner to use food without it becoming problematic."

Initially, however, food can be used in teaching target training. Davis offers this step-by-step guide:

1. Put double-sided tape to a plastic coffee lid and attach it to a door 2 feet above the floor.

2. Coat the center of the lid with liquid from a hot dog package to lure your dog to it.

3. Each time your dog touches the target's center with her nose, click and treat.

4. Remove the lid from the wall and hold it in your hand. Click and treat each time your dog's nose touches the center.

5. Move the lid up and down and then side to side, encouraging your dog to touch her nose to it in each position. Click and reward each time your dog touches the center.

6. Add distractions, such as noises, so that your dog learns to focus on the lid and ignore the distractions.

Teaching Specific Skills

Service dogs can perform a variety of tasks and can be custom trained to meet the specific needs of their owners. In this section, Davis will explain how target training can be used to close a door or drawer, open a door or drawer, *leave it*, fetch an object, and help make a bed.

CLOSE A DOOR

Rub a little treat on the center of a coffee lid and make sure that you have your clicker and several treats ready. Affix the lid to the outside center of a cupboard door. Each time your dog touches the lid, click and treat. Then open up the door a few inches. Allow your dog to move forward and touch the door with her nose. The door should move just a little bit. Click and treat the moment your dog touches the door hard enough with her nose or paw to move it.

You're ready to move to the next level. Refrain from clicking until your dog presses the lid target harder, moving the door more than just a bit. Open the door 1 inch and click, then 2 inches and click. Increase the width of the opening until the door is completely open. Attach a cue word, such as *push* or *close*, by saying the word just before you click but after

your dog has begun to move toward the door.

Once your dog knows how to close the cupboard door, try other doors in the house. Also try drawers, which take a bit more leverage. Remember to back up a bit, and lower your expectations when going to any new room. Just because your dog knows to press her nose on the door in the kitchen doesn't mean she will instantly close the bathroom door on cue.

OPEN A DOOR

When teaching your dog how to open a door, you need to first teach her how to *tug* or *pull* on cue. Davis recommends attaching a dishrag or piece of cloth to a cupboard or inside door. Playfully tease your dog to get her to grab and tug at the cloth. Place a treat inside the cupboard on a shelf and close the door. Attach a cloth to the outside of the door, wiggling it to entice your dog to grab and tug on it. This action will pull the door open a bit. When this happens, click and treat. As your dog gets the general idea, hold off on clicking until your dog begins to pull the door all the way open. Let her retrieve the treat from the shelf. Once your dog knows the door is part of the trick, remove

PHOTO BY TIM LOOSE

PHOTO BY DEBI DAVIS

the cloth and just let her target the door itself. Click and treat each time your dog paws or noses the cupboard door open.

Finally, attach a cue word, such as *open*, once the dog moves toward the door. Say the word right before you click. In time, your dog will begin to associate the command *open* with the act of opening up the door. Practice in different rooms of your home on various doors.

LEAVE IT

Service dogs must be very disciplined and resist temptations, such as food morsels on restaurant floors. To ensure that your dog ignores food or other distractions when out in public, Davis says you need to teach her the *leave it* cue.

At home, create two piles of food treats. Make one a high-valued food source, such as pieces of cheese or hot dog. Make the second pile of lesser value, such as pieces of dry kibble or plain cracker pieces. Place the high-valued treats on a table behind you and hold the low-valued treats in your hand. Extend your hand with the treats to your dog. Let her sniff it, but keep your fist closed so that she doesn't get any of the treats. The second she backs off, looks away, or ignores these treats, click and reward her with the pile of high-valued treats from the table behind you.

Repeat this until each time you hold out your hand with the low-valued treats, your dog quickly ignores them and looks to you. Your dog is learning to give up something in order to receive something of greater value, often referred to as doggy Zen in clicker-training circles. Now you're ready to open your hand to expose the kibble. Each time your dog ignores these treats, click and give her the tastier treats. Now, place a high-valued piece of treat in your hand, forming a fist if your dog mugs at your hand. As soon as she looks away, click and give her some treats from the table. Once your dog catches on to this game, add the cue word *leave it* just before you click, when your dog turns her head away from the treats in your hand. Lower the low-valued treats to the floor and repeat the word cue. Add a high-valued treat to this pile on the floor and ask your dog to *leave it*. Be sure to deliver the cue word in a neutral tone of voice, as it is a cue, not a punishment.

Finally, place all the treats on the floor. Put your dog on a leash and walk her by this pile, cuing her to *leave it* just as you both approach the treats. Reinforce the moment your dog ignores the pile by looking away. Click and treat.

FETCH AN OBJECT

Davis relies on Peekaboo to be her extra set of hands whenever she needs an object. In fact,

Peekaboo is so talented that he fetches small objects and brings them to Davis with the grace of a butler. Fetching is an essential behavior for service dogs, but it is a helpful one to teach to every dog. Your dog can bring you a magazine, a book, a cordless phone, or even the television remote control.

Natural or play retrieving ability is not necessary to teach your dog how to retrieve an object. Your dog must learn how to go to the object, pick it up, hold it gently, bring it to you, and sit until you ask her to release the object into your hand. Unlike teaching a dog to sit or stay, mastering the fetch command requires a sequence of ten steps. Rely on clicker training and build on each small success. Think of each step as links of a chain, with each link becoming strong enough to support the next link. Remember to ignore mistakes. Your dog will realize that if there's no click sound, she must try something else in order to get you to click and treat her.

To teach fetch in a fun way you will need:

- a pencil or dowel stick;
- tiny, soft treats the dog can quickly eat without having to chew;
- a clicker;
- a quiet, distraction-free room.

Ten Steps to Teaching Fetch.

1. Rub the treat on the center of a pencil or dowel stick to entice your dog to sniff it.

2. Sit down on the floor and hold the pencil out sideways to your dog. You are teaching your dog to touch the center part of the pencil. Click at the precise second her nose touches the pencil and immediately give her a treat. Repeat this several times, moving the pencil up and down, left and right.

3. Hold off on the click the next time she sniffs. She will offer a little more interaction to keep the game going, and your target behavior now is to get her to move the touch from her nose to her lips. You're looking to click and reward any kind of mouth action—a lick, a touch, a parting of the lips.

4. Once your dog puts her lips on the pencil each time you hold it out, hold off again to get her to offer a bit more action. She will most likely part her lips, or even part her

PHOTO BY TIM LOOSE

teeth, around the pencil. Click as this happens and quickly deliver the treat. Keep repeating this step, and click and reward only when your dog uses her mouth, not her nose.

5. Wait until your dog gets just a bit frustrated and presses her teeth on the pencil. Be ready to click at the same time the dog puts her teeth over the pencil. Repeat this several times, holding the pencil in different places.

6. Your dog now needs to learn that she must begin holding her teeth around the pencil for longer periods of time, until she hears the click. It's vital you don't move too quickly here or ask the dog to hold it for more than one second. You are literally teaching her a second at a time, extending the amount of time she holds it by seconds. Once your dog can hold the pencil for five seconds, move the pencil in different directions to help your dog feel comfortable. Remember that the click sound signals the end of the behavior, and it is okay if the pencil drops on the floor and you don't catch it. Your dog's job is over

once she hears the click. Click only when your dog holds the pencil solidly and quietly in her mouth.

7. Introduce a cue word or phrase, such as *let go* or *give*. To add this cue word, say the word just before you click. Your dog should now be able to pick up the pencil and hold it in her mouth for several seconds. Say, "Give," and immediately click and treat when your dog gives you the pencil. Hold the pencil in different directions and repeat the steps.

8. When you say, "Give," and your dog lets go of the pencil, add some distance. Hold the pencil closer and closer to the floor until it is finally resting on the floor. Practice having your dog pick up the pencil, hold it, and then give it to you on cue. You may have to click and treat for *any* movement your dog makes toward the pencil initially. Later, withhold the click until your dog has mastered holding the pencil in her mouth quietly until you give her the signal to drop it.

9. Add the *fetch* cue by waiting until your dog moves away from you to retrieve the

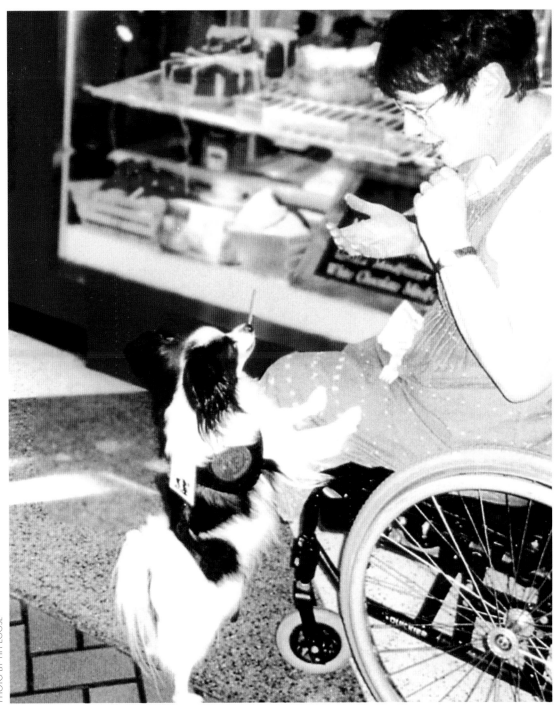

PHOTO BY TIM LOOSE

pencil. Say, "Fetch," as she is moving, and repeat this step several times to reinforce it. Your dog will begin to associate the command *fetch* with getting the pencil for you. Make sure that the aim of the game is accuracy not speed. Dogs in a hurry may not get a solid hold of the pencil and may spit it out in order to rush back out and do it again.

10. Expand this skill by practicing it in other rooms of the house. Gradually introduce light distractions so that your dog stays focused on the pencil and your cues. Once your dog is comfortable picking up the pencil in every room, no matter if you are sitting or standing, branch out. Have your dog fetch wood or soft plastic objects, such as hairbrushes or television remotes. Then introduce metal objects, such as car keys. Since metal objects are less appealing, you may need to recap the steps for sniffing, bumping, opening mouth, and holding. It won't take as long as the initial teaching, but you must have treats the dog really likes in order for her to put something in her mouth she doesn't like.

Final Tips. Teach your dog how to identify different objects to be fetched. Don't use similar sounding words such as *leash* and *keys* because the long "E" sound is very similar in each and can cause confusion in your dog. Teach names of items one at a time by attaching a name to the task, such as *fetch pencil* or *fetch remote*. If she picks up the wrong item, don't click or correct her, but don't accept the wrong object. Instead, let her drop it. The moment she selects the right item and puts it in her mouth, click and treat. If she drops it, fine. She doesn't have to bring it back to you, only select the right item at this point. Then, move around the house dropping other items in addition to a pencil but cue, "Fetch pencil." Once your dog can distinguish a pencil from other dropped objects, start adding other objects with the respective word cues to build up your dog's vocabulary.

HELP MAKE A BED

The two base behaviors needed to teach this task are:

1. Pull (tug object)
2. Back (move backward)

Teach your dog to tug on cue and release on cue. Once your dog consistently tugs each time you hold out a cloth, attach a cue word, such as *pull* or *tug*. The reward will be to continue the game. No food treats are necessary if your dog is a big fan of tug-of-war.

Now, you need to teach your dog to release the object on cue. One easy way is to stop pulling back and hold the cloth still. Many dogs will simply stop and release when there is no interaction. If you have an enthusiastic tugger, try blowing a little puff of air into her nose to make her release the object. Click at the moment of release and reward with praise or a treat. Once your dog knows the behavior of releasing the cloth, add the cue word *give* or *release* just as she releases the object. Repeat many times so that your dog will learn to associate the word with the desired behavior. Click and treat each successful time.

To teach your dog to back up, stand in front of her and take one step toward her. This should cause her to take a step back. The second she does, click and give a treat. Practice this until your dog is taking two, three, or more steps backward. Start attaching the cue word *back* just as she steps backward, and click and treat. Practice this in different rooms.

Now, head for the bed. Cue your dog to the foot of the bed (her head facing the foot of the bed). You should stand at the foot of the bed while your dog moves backward, up toward the head of the bed. Tell your dog to *pull* or *tug*. Your dog will start pulling the sheet and needs to continue backing up. If she doesn't, use the *back* cue to get her to move in the right direction. Practice patience and work slowly so that your dog does not become frustrated. Click and treat each time your dog takes a step or two backward with the corner of the sheet in her mouth. Cue her to release when she has tugged the sheet a few feet up toward the head of the bed. Once she consistently moves backward, tugging the sheet toward the head of the bed, switch to the other side of the bed and repeat these steps. Then introduce a blanket or bedspread to grab and pull. Finish with the pillows. Davis trains large dogs to work on the sides of the bed instead of being perched on the bed, but the training steps are the same.

AGING GRACEFULLY: TEACHING OLD DOGS NEW TRICKS

Profiled Trainer: Terry Ryan

Looking out the window of her classroom, third-grader Terry Ryan notices a dirty cocker spaniel-mix hanging around her schoolyard. Day after day, the homeless dog pays afternoon visits in hopes of getting some attention and maybe some treats from the school children. Desperately wanting a dog, the young Terry finally decides to lure this hungry dog home with pieces of her sandwich. But, as she climbed the concrete steps of her family's four-bedroom home in Glassboro, New Jersey, her father scowled his displeasure.

"My father was born in Sicily, where rabies was rampant among stray dogs. No way could I keep him, my father said. Then my four older brothers and sisters stepped in for me and convinced him otherwise," recalls Terry.

They named the dog Smokey. Smokey didn't earn high marks for obedience. He frequently dashed off the property, chasing neighbors' cats or tromping through vegetable gardens. He scored a new low the day he embarrassed the entire family. When the local priest came by to pick up collection money, Smokey

answered the knock on the door by promptly biting the priest on the foot. "I remember being mortified, but back then, we didn't know very much about raising a dog," says Terry. "Smokey lived to be eleven; he never learned any David Letterman-quality tricks, but I was just happy to have a dog." She and Smokey loved spending Friday nights watching episodes of *Rin Tin Tin*.

Terry's love for dogs led her to marry her high school sweetheart, Bill, whom she met at a county fair in Glassboro. "He reminded me of Jeff, the boy before Timmy, in the television show *Lassie*," says Terry. Exchanging wedding vows in 1966, the couple moved across the country to Albuquerque, New Mexico, sharing their home with a German shepherd named Honcho. Honcho proved to be much more trainable than Smokey. "We started training Honcho as a puppy, and he would fetch the newspaper and even place it on a specific table," recalls Terry. "Then, we would tell him it's time to go to bed, and he would cover himself up with a blanket and go nightie night—all these tricks he did without food treats—amazing." A neighbor who owned a poodle encouraged Terry to bring Honcho to a local dog obedience class. Terry accepted, seeing this as a chance to test Honcho's skills outside her home. Honcho graduated top dog, mastering every task quickly and easily, motivating Terry to enroll in more training classes, which eventually lead her to become an American Kennel Club obedience trial judge.

When Bill, a scientific glass blower, accepted a staff position at Washington State University, Terry landed a job as program coordinator for the dean of the university's veterinary school. Her engaging, creative teaching style drew notice, leading her to be chosen as program coordinator for the People Pet Partnership as well as affording her the opportunity to teach dog training overseas. "A woman from Japan observed my classes and invited me over to Japan—that was back in 1989, and I've been going back every year since," says Terry.

This former girl from New Jersey gained a global perspective into dog training—and an appreciation for different cultures. Not speaking Japanese didn't prove to be a drawback once Terry decided to think like a dog.

"Dog trainers are used to overcoming language barriers," says Terry. Every time we train a dog, we are running into the English as a Second Language problem with them. At least dogs have a universal language—body language—so if we are onto that, we are okay with dogs anywhere in the world...until we have to talk to their owners."

Now, she spends three or four months a year in Tochigi, Japan, as director of the Animal Fanciers School. She also conducts Japan's National Canine Good Citizen program and continuing education courses for Japan Guide Dogs. "Obviously, my first trip to Japan was a culture shock, but I believe Japan is the most exotic place on Earth—the places I've visited so far, anyway," she says. "Since 1989, I've noticed the bond between people and their dogs getting stronger. More dogs are with their owners in public places now." And, her Japanese language skills are constantly improving. She shares a few words commonly heard in Japanese dog classes: *Osuware!*—Sit! *Oide!*—Come! *Iiko!*—Good!

"Now I know enough Japanese to conduct a class, but I always read body language, both in dogs and their owners," she says.

Her skills led to the creation of not one but two businesses: Legacy Canine Behavior and Training, a business that conducts classes, seminars, and camps worldwide; and Legacy By Mail, a pet product mail order Web site company.

When she isn't globetrotting, she and her husband, and their cocker spaniel, Brody, enjoy their life in Sequim, Washington. Their home is filled with Aboriginal art—baskets, masks, and drums ("makes the house look like an anthropological museum")—situated on 6 acres frequently visited by herds of elk. Their living room windows open to a view of the Strait of Juan de Fuca, which empties into the Pacific Ocean where gray whales migrate. And, when reruns of *Lassie* or *Rin Tin Tin* appear on the television, you can bet the trio is attentively tuned in.

Introduction

Perhaps you adopted an older dog from your local shelter or discovered to your dismay that the dog you've raised developed into a four-legged Dennis the Menace. He seems to have forgotten all his basic obedience commands and turned into a new breed: *Canis obnoxious!* Contrary to popular myth, you can teach an old dog new tricks and refresh his memory on the basics in a fun, positive way. No need for brute force or an I'll-show-you-who's-boss mentality. In this chapter, Ryan will guide you toward honing your leadership skills and restoring harmony to your household. She has been helping dogs and their owners for three decades, literally all over the globe.

The first step in retooling your problem dog begins with you. Sometimes dogs behave in less-than-ideal ways because owners fail to project themselves as leaders of the household pack or are inconsistent in their commands. One time it's okay for your dog to lounge on the couch, but when company arrives, suddenly the couch is off-limits. It can be quite confusing to a dog. Establish a household hierarchy with you as the leader and teacher. Be kind and

consistent in your leadership and your dog will feel safe knowing that you are in charge. Dogs learn by association. Naturally, a dog is apt to repeat an action such as digging in the yard when it leads to a satisfying result: getting cool during a hot summer day. This is one of the many principles of operant conditioning.

The principle states that if an action leads to a satisfying result, the action is likely to be repeated. Ryan recommends using this principle to your advantage. If you say, "Cosmo, come," and each time he responds, you praise and pet him, he is likely to obey, perhaps even quicker the next time you call for him.

However, if you call for your dog and then yell at him for tipping over the kitchen garbage can or chasing the neighbor's cat, he may be less likely to heed your *come* command the next time.

Take a Ride on the YES TRAIN

Now, let's tackle this business of getting your older dog back on track. Ryan's training approach to unwanted behaviors, such as barking, can be summarized by the acronym YES TRAIN, which stands for:

Yield a Little

Eliminate the Cause

Systematic Desensitization

Take Away the Reward for the Bad Behavior

Reward an Incompatible Behavior

Acclimate the Dog

Improve the Dog's Association

Not Much Nasty Stuff

Ryan refers to her "toolbox" concept when retraining dogs to behave appropriately. It is important to have many tools at your disposal when reshaping your dog's behavior; it is equally important to recognize the right tool for the job. For example, if you need to put a screw into a wall, which tool would be most appropriate: a hammer or a screwdriver? Technically, you could bang a screw into the wall with a hammer, but the screw wouldn't stay in place for long. You could also end up creating another problem—punching a hole into the wall, which would need to be repaired. Apply this select-the-right tool concept to dog training.

For more details, let's take a YES TRAIN trip with Ryan as our conductor.

YIELD A LITTLE

Effective dog owners quickly see the value in striking compromises with their canine chums. No need to completely cave in to your dog's wishes, but giving in a little can often improve your living arrangement. Ryan notes that compromising appeals to owners with limited time or talent to train their older dogs. And, she says that yielding a little works well when combined with other training techniques. However, never compromise for problems that might endanger people or your dog. If your dog is showing aggressive tendencies, for instance, seek professional help from your veterinarian, dog trainer, or animal behaviorist.

Let's say you have a bone to pick with your dog because of his barking. Try compromising by allowing your dog to bark in the side yard far away from neighbors or let him enjoy three free barks before you step in and tell him to be quiet.

ELIMINATE THE CAUSE

Dogs often have a good reason for doing what they do. Play dog detective and try to pinpoint the cause behind the unwanted behavior. An older dog who suddenly starts urinating on the living room carpet may be suffering from a kidney or bladder disease, or some other medical condition. A dog who ignores your calls may have an ear infection, deafness, or the early onslaught of cognitive dysfunction syndrome, a relatively new condition that is the doggy equivalent to dementia. He may simply feel lost, or even like a stranger in his own house. When in doubt, have your dog examined by your veterinarian to rule out an underlining medical cause.

Let's say your dog is deemed physically fit but continues to bark excessively. Try to determine when your dog barks. Is there a pattern, such as only during thunderstorms or on Monday mornings? When did his barking pattern begin—since puppy hood or recently? Did it start after you moved into a new home, returned from a long vacation, or after your daughter left for college? Where does your dog bark? Inside, outside, or both? Does he bark at everything and anyone or just at a specific person or object? Ryan recommends that you document the barking patterns by writing them down on a notepad. Ask neighbors or other family members to note the barking when you're not home, or try leaving a tape recorder on. Perhaps you will discover that your dog has a medical condition that needs attention, or that he barks out of boredom or separation anxiety from being home alone more than usual. Eliminating the cause resolves specific barking issues, but it may not alter your dog's attitude toward other similar situations. Your dog may stop barking at the mail carrier

because you now make sure he is with you in the kitchen around mail time, but this won't resolve the issue of your dog barking when an unscheduled delivery arrives.

SYSTEMATIC DESENSITIZATION

Time to think—and act—like a psychologist.

Set up a training session in which the triggers causing the barking are presented at very low levels and watch your dog very carefully for signals that he is about to bark. Gradually increase the stimuli, striving to avoid triggering your dog's reaction. Continue until your dog is able to cope with the problem stimuli.

But go slowly. If you proceed too swiftly, you risk overwhelming and confusing your dog. Ryan explains this tactic by providing this example of an owner clearly communicating with her dog: "Freddy, I wish you wouldn't bark every time you see me pick up your leash for a walk. We're going to work on this together. At first, I will only look at your leash. If you're quiet, I'm going to pick up your leash several times a day. Sometimes I'll just put it back, sometimes I'll hook it to your collar and then take it off and put it back, and once in a while we'll go for a walk."

TAKE AWAY THE REWARD
FOR THE BAD BEHAVIOR

This training tactic, known in psychological terms as extinction, avoids confrontations and is easy, requiring very little time, effort, or skill to master. You must first recognize that most behaviors are maintained by rewards. Some rewards are so subtle that your dog notices them, but you do not. So, once you identify the reward that sustains the unwanted behavior—barking—and eliminate it, chances are the behavior will decrease.

Let's say that your dog barks in the backyard when people pass by. Each time, you go out the back door and holler, "Shut up!" Your actions are rewarding to your dog because he feels that he has figured out a way to get you to pay more attention to him. When he barks, you react. Try ignoring him and see if the barking lessens. More likely, the barking will temporarily worsen. Ryan says this transient increase in behavior is to be expected. For ultimate success, you need to be patient and stick it out. The barking will eventually lessen when you use the extinction-training tactic.

To illustrate this point, Ryan gives the example of a young child insisting that his mother give him a cookie:

"Mom, I want a cookie."

"Not now, Billy."

"But I want a cookie N-O-W!" says Billy, as he begins stomping his feet.

Billy's mom ignores his verbal and physical outbursts, and eventually, the boy will give up.

Victory to Mom.

"With your dog, let's face it, it might be impossible to ignore the barking dog due to complaints from your neighbors who are threatening to contact the local animal control officer," says Ryan. "Or, more importantly, you are not taking away the cause behind the barking. You need to consider from the dog's point of view what is upsetting him or causing him to bark."

REWARD AN INCOMPATIBLE BEHAVIOR

Emotionally speaking, dogs can't feel happy and sad at the same time. It's impossible. Apply this knowledge by training and rewarding your dog for a behavior that is incompatible with an unacceptable one.

Let's say your highly energetic dog likes to bound out the front door the second it is opened just a crack. To counter this inappropriate behavior, have your dog get into the sit position each time that you reach for the doorknob. The action of sitting while the door is open is incompatible with your dog's action of dashing out the door.

The second your dog gets out of the sit position and tries to scoot out as the door starts to open, counter this by simply shutting the door. Your dog will learn that it is better to patiently sit at the door rather than bully his way through.

ACCLIMATE THE DOG

Ryan isn't referring to the weather in this training tip. Instead, she is referring to habituation—exposing a dog to an identified problem-producing stimulus in a safe, supervised setting so that over time, he gets used to it. This technique is time-consuming but is especially effective for fearful or overly excited dogs. Perhaps your dog panics when you bring out the vacuum cleaner. Ryan recommends that you leave the vacuum cleaner (turned off) in the living room. With the absence of any reward or punishment, let your dog investigate this appliance and retreat at will. By creating a neutral environment, your frightened dog will eventually realize that there is nothing to fear and calm down.

IMPROVE THE DOG'S ASSOCIATION

Psychologists call this step counterconditioning because it pairs something unpleasant with something of high value. Dogs have great memories, which makes this training method crucial to changing your dog's behavior. Maybe your dog hates riding in the car because he associates the car with a dreaded trip to the veteri-

nary clinic or staying overnight at the boarding kennel. This is where you step in and pair something of high value to the dog—a trip to the local dog park or a visit to your dog-loving parents' home—with the problem stimulus: the car. Instead of always equating the car with unpleasant activities, your dog will associate it with fun activities.

NOT MUCH NASTY STUFF

Slapping, swatting with a rolled up newspaper, jerking on the leash, screaming, shaking, and pinning a dog to the floor seldom work, and are harmful and hurtful. Sure, these actions may interrupt the bad behavior for a second or two, but rarely do these forms of punishment provide a permanent fix.

Can't stop your barking dog? Yelling, hitting your dog, or yanking on his collar may stop the barking, but Ryan says these actions can often worsen a dog's fear response and heighten his level of anxiety. "If a dog is worried and barks at the mail carrier and you scream and holler at your dog to be quiet," says Ryan. "What you might have unintentionally done is make the dog start to worry about both the mail carrier and you."

The use of physical punishment can come back to haunt you by giving your dog the wrong message. Let's say your dog starts pulling on the leash to check out an approaching person. In response, you jerk hard on the leash and yell, "Bad dog!" Your dog may either read that to mean he is being bad for pulling on the leash or that the person he wanted to approach is bad. Some dogs actually perceive punishment as a reward. If your dog barks when you host your weekly Scrabble party and you banish him to the back den, your dog may think, *Great, finally a place of safety. Now I know how to act the next time I want to get away from these visitors.*

Finally, using unnecessary force can signifi-cantly harm the friendship bond and level of trust between you and your dog. He may start to view your hand as a foe, not a friend.

Quick Fix Tools

Unlike choke collars or pinch collars, the head collar is a gentle and effective tool to correct unwanted behaviors such as excessive barking or leash pulling by your dog during daily walks. "If you control the head, you control the dog," says Ryan. "A head collar does not put pressure on your dog's throat. The most effective type of head collar fits up higher and rests on the jawbones to give you physical control without hurting your dog. It also gives you psychological control because most dogs recognize the muzzle strap as an extension of your leadership and often settle into a more mellow mood once they are wearing it."

During a walk, increase your popularity in the mind of your dog. If you have a dog who seems more interested in sniffing the trash in the gutter than heeling by your side, rely on food treats or toys as your allies. Before you head out for a walk, stash a few yummy treats or your dog's favorite toy in your jacket.

Use a head halter to gently and effectively correct unwanted behaviors such as barking.

Periodically call your dog by name during your stroll. When he pays attention to you, give him a treat or play a quick game of fetch. Then continue the walk. This will increase your "curb appeal" over the trash in the gutter or any other distractions during your walk together.

Cures for the Home-Alone Dog

Owners can sidestep misbehaviors triggered by separation anxiety by creating a happy, safe, and fun home for their home-alone dog, says Ryan. She offers these simple strategies to turn your home into a haven for your dog during your absence:

DOG TRAINING, A LIFELONG GUIDE

- **Doggy-proof your place.** Think of your dog as a curious human toddler. Go through your home, room by room, and look for any items that may harm your dog. Prevent accidental poisoning by installing childproof plastic latches on kitchen and bathroom cabinet doors, moving plants out of reach, and not allowing your dog access to the garage where he can lick spilled antifreeze. Keep the lid down on toilets and keep candy jars, loose coins, and jewelry out of paw's reach.

- **Bring on the food feast.** A few minutes before you head out the door for work, give your dog a hollow, hard rubber, chewable toy, stuffed with his favorite regular food plus a dab of his favorite treat. Among the choices to consider: a dab of peanut butter, cream cheese, mashed bananas, or pieces of rice cake. Your dog will be so busy getting every little morsel out that he won't notice your absence for hours. This tactic helps curb destructiveness, overeager greeting, and separation anxiety tendencies. Clean these rubber toys in your dishwasher or with hot soapy water at least once a week.

- **Avoid emotion-filled departures and arrivals.** Whenever you leave and return home, do so without a lot of fanfare. Often, owners unintentionally create separation anxiety in their dogs because they make a big deal of departures, *I'm so sorry I have to go work today, Foxi,* or returns, *Hey Foxi! Guess who's home?* Give your dog a treat or activity before you leave, and purposely spend five to ten minutes when you return home checking your mail or listening to your phone messages before addressing your dog. He will learn to wait patiently for your undivided attention.

- **Set up a food scavenger hunt.** Most dogs love to be assigned jobs. Teach your dog the *find the treat* command. First, hide treats in clear view and encourage your dog to retrieve them, saying, "Find the Treat," delivering plenty of praise when he finds them. As your dog gets the idea of the game, start placing treats in less visible places. Finally, stash some food treats around your house—behind a chair, under the coffee table, on the top stair—for your dog to find after you leave for work each morning.

- **Paging Fido.** Dogs love the sound of their

owner's voice. Consider telephoning home twice a day and leaving a spirited message for your dog, such as *Hey, Spot, this is Barbara. I'll be home in a couple hours and I look forward to taking you on a long walk.* Or, record the next family dinner conversation or evening get-together. Set the tape recorder so that it replays continuously or put it on a timer during the day. Nothing is more depressing than the sound of silence to a dog. Your tape provides him with auditory stimulation.

- **Muffle noise distractions.** Consider turning on the radio or the television to filter out unpleasant sounds, such as the neighbor's yapping dog, traffic, or even thunderstorms.

- **Make crates homes, not prisons.** A dog should never be kept in a crate longer than four hours. Crates should be regarded as dens that offer privacy and protection for your dog. If you keep your dog in a crate for eight hours or more, he will no longer see the crate as a refuge but more as a prison and start exhibiting inappropriate behaviors. Until your dog earns run of the house, limit his access to areas such as easy-to-clean rooms like the kitchen or living room (if free of carpeting) that can be blocked off with see-through doggy gates.

- **Create dog havens throughout the house.** Does your dog love to snooze on your sofa? Compromise by placing a bed sheet or washable throw blanket on top of the cushions. When you come home, remove the sheet and reclaim your fur-free sofa. Also, place dog beds or blankets in a few places around the house where there is sunshine and solitude.

- **Provide mental and physical exercise outlets.** A lot of destructive behavior is due to a bored dog or one who receives inadequate amounts of exercise, says Ryan. So schedule at least twenty minutes of exercise before you go to work to walk your dog. When you take your dog out on a walk, don't bring him back in as soon as he goes to the bathroom. Add some spice to the walk by spending some time practicing such commands as *heel*, *sit*, and *roll over*. Use this time together to reinforce your dog's mental focus, giving him a good workout so that when he comes inside, he is ready to relax or take a nap.

- **Offer bathroom outlets.** Depending on your home and the behavior of your dog, consider installing doggy doors that permit access to fenced-in outdoor areas or doggy litter boxes. If those options aren't feasible, make arrangements in advance with friends or neighbors to provide bathroom breaks for your dog if you will arrive home later than usual.

- **Vary the daily routine.** Treat your dog to an occasional day at a doggy day care center or a midday visit from a dog-friendly neighbor or professional pet-sitter. Make sure that the doggy centers and pet-sitters are trained, insured, and bonded.

ON-TARGET SOLUTIONS
FOR COMMON DOGGY MISDEEDS

Inappropriate Chewing: Your dog destroys your wallet, television remote control, shoes, socks, or other prized possessions.

Quick Remedy: Become a tidier housekeeper. Store wallets and socks in dresser drawers, remotes on high shelves, and shoes in closets with doors or in rooms closed off with baby gates. Divert your dog's need to chew toward "legal" chew objects, such as a hollow rubber Kong toy or nylon bone.

Leash Yanking: Your dog drags you on your walks as he lunges after squirrels, cats, or other dogs.

Quick remedy: Train him to walk with manners by the use of a head collar. The head collars are more effective and humane than choke or pinch collars. The halters allow you to control your dog's head, which, in turn, controls his body direction. During walks, reward your dog any time there is slack in the leash. Refuse to continue the walk when he starts to pull.

Garden Digging: No need to sacrifice your rose bush or strawberry patch to your dog's desire to find China with his determined digging.

Quick Remedy: First, protect your garden area by installing a low but sturdy fence to make it off-limits to your dog. Then provide a sandbox with occasional buried treats or toys for your dig-happy dog. Also consider installing a dog run or outdoor kennel. You can purchase a premade steel-and-wire dog run from many pet supply stores.

Trashcan Tipping: The smell of last night's fried chicken dinner scraps in the kitchen garbage can be simply too irresistible to your dog, so much so you discover him head deep into the can with trash strewn across the floor.

Quick Remedy: Take away the temptation by keeping the trashcan and its smelly treasures out of paw's reach. Store the trash bin in the cabinet under the sink and install a childproof latch on the cabinet doors. Or, buy a trashcan with a snap-on lid, or clamp down the lid using bungee cords. You can also stow the trashcan inside an attached garage or install a baby gate in your kitchen doorway to block your dog's access.

Lounging on Furniture: Does your hairy dog love to stretch out on your sofa, drape himself over your recliner, or take over the loveseat?

Quick Remedy: Turn recliners upside down and place them up against walls while you're away from home. Place a cookie sheet on a chair to make it less inviting. Or, compromise by placing a washable blanket or sheet over the furniture to allow your dog to snooze with comfort. Remove the covering when you return home at night.

Dog Attacks the Vacuum Cleaner: In some dogs, the prey drive takes center stage when you bring out the vacuum cleaner, water hose, lawn mower, or other appliance.

Quick Remedy: Put your dog in another part of your home before you begin using the targeted appliance. Keep him inside an enclosed room or one with a baby gate. To desensitize your dog to these appliances, slowly increase your dog's exposure to them. First, expose your dog to the appliances with them turned off and at a distance. Then, gradually move the appliances closer and closer. Eventually turn them on in your dog's presence. Reward him with food treats and praise each time he remains calm around them.

Leaps to Greet: You may have thought it was cute when your 4-pound puppy jumped on people when they walked in the front door, but now your puppy grew into an overly excited 50-pound adult who is knocking over visitors.

Quick Remedy: Train your dog to sit automatically at the door when greeting people. Start by putting a leash on your dog and standing on the middle of the leash so your dog cannot jump up. Give your arriving guests dog treats to give to your dog only when he is sitting. Praise and treat your dog for not jumping.

Appendix A

★ ★ ★ ★ ★ ★ ★ ★ ★ ★ ★

TIPS ON CHOOSING A DOG TRAINER AND TRAINING CLASS

★ ★ ★ ★ ★ ★ ★ ★ ★ ★ ★

Choosing a Dog Trainer

You've just witnessed your first agility dog event and now you want to compete. Maybe you just adopted a puppy and want to get her off on the right paw by enrolling her in a top-notch puppy kindergarten class. Or, you have a dog who needs a refresher course in manners and obedience. You're eager to enroll in a dog training class but where and with whom?

"You'll need to do your homework to make sure that you find a trainer who is current with reward-based training techniques," advises Terry Long, a professional dog agility trainer and managing editor of the Association of Professional Dog Trainers (APDT) newsletter from Long Beach, California.

According to Long, a skilled dog trainer will:
- provide a clear explanation of each lesson, answering the how as well as the why;
- demonstrate the behavior being taught by using a trained dog or a dog in the class first so the class can see how to do the exercise;

- distribute written handouts that provide step-by-step instructions on how to practice with a dog at home;
- use positive reinforcement to direct the owner and his or her dog to the appropriate behavior or technique.

Long recommends selecting a trainer based on the following:

- **Assess the class environment for safety.** Beginners' classes, for instance, should cover the basics in a fun, cooperative approach and not require dogs to perform advance or complex commands. The location should provide adequate lighting if indoors and shade if outdoors. The ground should be free of hazards such as tree roots above ground and holes.

- **Check out the instructor's credentials.** The best professional dog trainers own dogs and are among the nation's top performance sport competitors or obedience participants. Seek an instructor who has titled his or her dog(s) and keeps current on training methods by enrolling in continuing education programs, or serves as an agility judge.

- **Observe two or three classes before enrolling.** Qualified trainers actually encourage individuals considering their classes to watch a few from the sidelines. Attend the first class without your dog so that you can devote your full attention to watching how the trainer motivates people and their dogs, the mood of the class, and the level of interaction between the students and the trainer. Then bring your dog on a leash to the class and watch together. Watching the class beforehand gives you an idea of the physical demands required for both the handler and the dog.

- **Take note of the class size and duration.** The class should be limited in size so that you get ample time to practice new techniques with your dog instead of wasting time standing around waiting for your turn. Classes should be limited to ninety minutes or less to maintain a dog's focus.

- **Interview the trainer.** Before deciding on a specific instructor, find out what training methods they use and why. An instructor's training style should match yours. Avoid trainers who rely on negative techniques, such as yanking on choke chains or leashes, and sidestep those who "guarantee" results. A good trainer should be willing to spend twenty minutes or more with you without any interruptions, communicate well, and clearly convey tips and techniques to students. If a trainer can't communicate well with people, keep looking for a trainer who can. Finally, get the names of current and former students, and ask them what they liked and disliked about the trainer.

- **Trust your dog's instincts.** Dog classes require a partnership between you and your dog, and your dog and the trainer. Your dog must like the trainer in order to learn. Good signs: your dog rushes to greet the trainer with a back wiggle and wide-tail sweeping motions. Bad signs: your dog crouches and tucks her tail each time the trainer approaches.

WALK AWAY IF A DOG TRAINER DOES ANY OF THE FOLLOWING...

Recommends you put a choke chain on your dog to correct an unwanted behavior or action. Pain-induced learning can harm your dog.

Advises you to yank sharply on your dog's leash to stop an unwanted action.

Tells you to pin your dog on her back and hover over her in a dominating stance. This can actually backfire and lead to aggression in some dogs.

Insists on removing your dog from your home and teaching her one-on-one without your presence.

Obtained his or her credentials through mail order courses or misrepresents himself or herself with bogus or misleading credentials.

Choosing a Training Class

Resist the temptation to sign up for the first class you find or one that is simply closest to your home. Select one that best meets you and your dog's needs.

When you're observing the class, pay attention to your surroundings and take note of the following:

- **Location:** Is the class held inside a clean, spacious setting or inside a cramped, dirty, or noisy room? Is the location equipped to maintain a cool temperature in the summer and warmth in the winter? Are there convenient trashcans and potty areas with clean-up sup-plies readily available?

- **Size of the class:** Does there seem to be too few or too many dogs? Are you comfortable with the ratio of instructors to dogs? Do you feel that your dog would receive enough one-on-one attention?

- **Size of the dogs:** Are there enough big and small dogs to help your dog realize that dogs come in many shapes and sizes?

- **Age of the class:** Experts recommend that puppy classes be limited to puppies under six months of age.

- **Auxiliary help:** Does one trainer who also tries to handle all of the administrative chores direct the class?

- **Length of the class:** Dogs are notorious for having short attention spans. Are there scheduled breaks? One-hour classes with one or two short breaks are ideal.

- **Training style:** Is the training approach encour-aging and positive or is it one in which faults are pointed out and accomplishments are ignored? Does the trainer spell out the whys behind different activities and offer easy, step-by-step instructions? Can you easily apply these techniques inside your home and when you are outside with your dog or puppy?

- **Class agenda:** Is there time allotted at the begin-ning of class for playtime so that the dogs can mingle and unleash some energy before the core learning begins? Does the training take a fun approach to teaching basic commands, such as *sit, stay,* and *look at me*? Is time set aside to allow owners to ask questions? Does the trainer provide handouts at the end of class?

- **Family affair:** Does the trainer encourage owners to bring in their children and other dog caregivers to participate or is it limited to just one owner per dog?

- **Listen to comments:** Do owners appear relaxed and look like they are enjoying the class? Are their comments positive or nega-tive when they leave class?

Appendix B

* * * * * * * * * *

PROFILED TRAINERS

* * * * * * * * * *

Deb Davis, service-dog trainer,
Tucson, Arizona.
Web site: www.clickertales.com
E-mail: Scripto@azstarnet.com

Donna Duford, owner of Companion Dog
Training School, San Francisco, California.
E-mail: donnaduford@aol.com

Susan Garrett
2780 Dunmark Road
Alberton, Ontario.
Canada LOR 1AO
Web site: www.clickerdogs.com
E-mail: susan@clickerdogs.com

Terry Ryan, president of Legacy Canine
Behavior and Training, Inc., Sequim,
Washington.
Web site: www.legacycanine.com
E-mail: teryan@olypen.com

Sue Sternberg, director of Rondout Valley
Kennels, Inc. and professional dog trainer,
Accord, New York.
Web site: www.suesternberg.com
E-mail: suecarmen@aol.com

Appendix C

* * * * * * * * * * *

TIPS ON CHOOSING AND FINDING A BEHAVIORAL CONSULTANT

* * * * * * * * * * *

Choosing a Behavioral Consultant

When you need one-on-one professional training to modify your dog's behaviors or when training issues become too complex for you to handle, consult a professional animal behaviorist.

Definitely seek professional help if your dog:
* growls, snaps, or gives you a stony stare when you touch him, stand over him, try to get him off of a resting place, or when you get near his food or toys;
* lunges at, chases, nips, or bites other people or animals, or seems unduly afraid of anything in the environment.

In selecting a behavioral consultant, choose an individual who:
* uses positive methods;

- makes no promises or guarantees;
- agrees to see your dog in person;
- offers references.

How to Find a Behavioral Consultant

Following are organizations that can help you find a qualified behavioral consultant near you:

Animal Behavior Society

c/o Steve Zawistowski, Ph.D., ASPCA

424 E. 92nd Street

New York, NY 10128

(212) 876-7700, ext. 4401

Web site: www.animalbehavior.org

E-mail: stevez@aspca.org

American College of Veterinary Behaviorists

Bonnie Beaver, D.V.M., executive director and professor in the Department of Small Animal Medicine and Surgery

Texas A & M University

College Station, TX 77843-4474

(409) 845-3195

E-mail: bbeaver@vetmed.tamu.edu

American Veterinary Society of Animal Behavior

Laurie Martin, D.V.M., secretary-treasurer.

201 Cedarbrook Road

Naperville, IL 60565

(630) 983-7749 or (630) 759-0093

E-mail: martinala@juno.com

Appendix D

★ ★ ★ ★ ★ ★ ★ ★ ★

RESOURCES

★ ★ ★ ★ ★ ★ ★ ★ ★

Associations

American Humane Association

Provides education on pet care to owners, shelters, and the veterinary community.

63 Iverness Drive East

Englewood, CO 80112

(303) 925-9453

Web site: www.americanhumane.org

American Kennel Club

5580 Centerview Drive, Suite 200

Raleigh, NC 27606

(919) 233-9767

For agility information check the Web site:

www.akc.org

E-mail: agility@akc.org

American Society for the Prevention of Cruelty to Animals (ASPCA)

424 E. 92nd Street

New York, NY 10128

(212) 876-7700

Web site: www.aspca.org

E-mail: website@aspca.org

The Association of Pet Dog Trainers

Founded in 1983 by Ian Dunbar, Ph.D., D.V.M. Dedicated to promoting good trainers through education.

17000 Commerce Parkway, Suite C

Mt. Laurel, NJ 08054

(800) PET-DOGS

Fax: (856) 439-0525

Web site: www.apdt.com

Canine Freestyle Federation

4207 Minton Drive

Fairfax, VA 22032

(703) 323-7216

Web site: www.canine-freestyle.org

E-mail: president@canine-freestyle.org

Delta Society

Provides medical research on the benefits
of companion animals and trains
therapy animals.

289 Perimeter Road East

Renton, WA 98055

(800) 869-6898

Web site: www.deltasociety.org

Friskies ALPO Canine Frisbee Disc

Sponsors regional and national flying
disc contests.

4060-D Peachtree Road, Suite 326

Atlanta, GA 30319

(800) 786-9240

Web site: www.skyhoundz.com

E-mail: info@skyhoundz.com

Humane Society of the United States

Ranks as the world's largest animal
protection organization.

2100 L Street, NW

Washington, DC 20037

(202) 452-1100

Web site: www.hsus.org

International Disc Dog Handlers Association

Web site: www.iddha.com

E-mail: IDDHA@aol.com

National Association of Dog Obedience Instructors

Contact Corresponding Secretary

729 Grapevine Hwy, Suite 369

Hurst, TX 76054-2085

www.nadoi.org

North American Dog Agility Council

11550 South Hwy 3

Cataldo, ID 83810

Fax: (209) 689-3906

Web site: www.nadac.com

E-mail: info@nadac.com

North American Flyball Association

1400 W. Devon Ave., Box 512

Chicago, IL 60660

(309) 688-4915

E-mail: melmcavoy@worldnet.att.net

Bob Long, tournament director,

(619) 571-7022 or E-mail: boblong@cts.com

United States Dog Agility Association

P.O. Box 850955

Richardson, TX 75085

(972) 487-2200

Web site: www.usdaa.com

E-mail: info@usdaa.com

World Canine Freestyle Organization

Patie Ventre, founder

P.O. Box 350122

Brooklyn, NY 11235

(718) 332-5238

Web site: www.woofs.org

E-mail: wcfodogs@aol.com

Books and Brochures

Donaldson, Jean. 1997. *The Culture Clash.* Berkeley, Calif.: James and Kenneth Publishers.

Donaldson, Jean. 1998. *Dogs are from Neptune.* Montreal, Quebec: Lasar Multimedia Productions, Inc.

Duford, Donna. 1999. *Agility Tricks For Improved Attention, Flexibility and Confidence.* North Brookfield, Mass.: Clean Run Productions.

Dunbar, Ian, Ph.D, D.V.M. 1998. *How to Teach a New Dog Old Tricks*. Berkeley, Calif.: James and Kenneth Publishers.

Garrett, Susan. 2002. *Ruff Love: A Relationship Building Program*. North Brookfield, Mass.: Clean Run Productions.

Kilcommons, Brian, and Sarah Wilson. 1999. *Paws to Consider: Choosing the Right Dog for You and Your Family*. New York: Warner Books.

Moore, Arden. 2000. *50 Simple Ways to Pamper Your Dog*. North Adams, Mass.: Storey Books.

Moore, Arden. 2001. *Real Food for Dogs*. North Adams, Mass.: Storey Books.

Pryor, Karen. 1999. *Don't Shoot the Dog: The New Art of Teaching and Training*. New York: Bantam Books.

Ryan, Terry. 1998. *The Toolbox for Remodeling Your Problem Dog*. New York: Howell Book House.

Ryan, Terry. 2000. *The Bark Stops Here*. Sequim, Wash.: Legacy By Mail.

Sternberg, Sue. 1999. *Sue Sternberg Presents a Guide to Choosing Your Next Dog from the Shelter*. Accord, NY: Rondout Valley Kennels, Inc. To order, phone: (914) 687-7619; e-mail: suecarmen@aol.com; or write to: 4628 Route 209, Accord, NY 12404

Sternberg, Sue. 2000a. *Temperament Testing for Dogs in Shelters*. Accord, NY: Rondout Valley Kennels, Inc. To order, phone: (914) 687-7619; e-mail: suecarmen@aol.com; or write to: 4628 Route 209, Accord, NY 12404

Sternberg, Sue. 2000b. *Training for Dogs in Shelters*. Accord, NY: Rondout Valley Kennels, Inc. To order, phone: (914) 687-7619; e-mail: suecarmen@aol.com; or write to: 4628 Route 209, Accord, NY 12404

Publications

The Clicker Journal

A magazine for animal trainers.

4040 Rosewell Plantation Road

Gloucester, VA 23061

Dog Fancy magazine

P.O. Box 6050

Mission Viejo, CA 92618-2804

(949) 855-8822

Web site: www.dogfancy.com

Videos

Sirius Puppy Training with Ian Dunbar. 1987. Produced by Bluford/Toth Productions. James and Kenneth Publishers. To order, call: (800) 784-5531.

Training Your Shelter Dog by Sue Sternberg. Produced by Nabisco-Milk Bone & ASPCA. To order, send $3.90 by check or money order to: Milk Bone, Consumer and Scientific Affairs, 100 DeForest Avenue, P.O. Box 1911, East Hanover, NJ 07936.

TERMINOLOGY

a-frame: a large contact obstacle with two ramps that meet at a peak in the center and has a width of 3 to 4 feet.

agility course: an obstacle course for dogs.

clicker training: a training method that breaks down exercises or behaviors into small increments and rewards them with a clicking noise a handler makes from squeezing a palm-sized clicking device each time a dog performs correctly.

contact obstacle: a yellow painted stripe (known as a contact) within an obstacle that a dog must step on or leap over in order to stay penalty-free during a competition.

counterconditioning: conditioning in order to replace an undesirable response (fear) to a stimulus (a visit to the veterinarian's office) by a favorable one (a trip to the park).

desensitization: a technique used to make a sensitized or hypersensitive dog insensitive or nonreactive to a sensitizing agent (vacuum cleaner).

dog walk: a tall obstacle that has two ramps joined by a long plank.

intact: a dog who has not been spayed or neutered.

operant conditioning: conditioning in which the desired behavior (*come*) is followed by a rewarding or reinforcing stimulus (a click or treat).

pylon: a post or tower marking a prescribed course.

service dog: a dog who is specially trained to work with people who have limited mobility.

shaping: to modify (behavior) by rewarding changes that tend toward a desired response.

target training: a method used in training assistance tasks where the goal is to teach your dog to touch an object with his nose or paw.

weave poles: six to twelve poles set 18 to 25 inches apart in a straight line. The dog must enter them right to left and weave through them.

For more authoritative and helpful facts about dogs, including health-care advice, grooming tips, and insights into the special joys—and overcoming the unique problems—of dog ownership, check out the latest copy of *Dog Fancy* magazine or visit the Web site at www.dogfancy.com.

BowTie™ Press is a division of Fancy Publications, which is the world's largest publisher of pet magazines. For more books on dogs, look for *Barking, Chewing, House-Training, Digging, Dogs Are Better Than Cats, Dogs Rule!, The Splendid Little Book of All Things Dog, Why Do Dogs Do That? and Puppies! Why Do They Do What They Do?* You can find all these books and more at www.bowtiepress.com.